A LONELY MINORITY

A Lonely Minority

The Modern Story of Egypt's Copts

BY EDWARD WAKIN

AN AUTHORS GUILD BACKINPRINT.COM EDITION

AN AUTHORS GUILD BACKINPRINT.COM EDITION

Published by iUniverse.com, Inc.

For information address:
iUniverse.com, Inc.
620 North 48th Street, Suite 201
Lincoln, NE 68504-3467
www.iuniverse.com

Originally published by William Morrow

Revised with a new dedication and preface

ISBN: 0-595-08914-3

Printed in the United States of America

To my grandsons, Thomas and Michael

Contents

List of Illustrations
(between pages 102-103)

PREFACE

On a weekday morning in downtown Cairo, a Jesuit priest in white cassock was rushing into a car on the way to an appointment when he was handed a note. He read it quickly, shook hands briskly and made a date to meet, then hurried away. As always, he was on the move, except for his daily meditation in the afternoon when he stopped, wherever he was, to pray.

The note, signed by a Vatican official assigned to Middle Eastern affairs, introduced this writer and asked the Jesuit to assist in my research on the struggle to survive by the millions of Christians comprising the Coptic minority of Egypt. (Today, they number at least six million.)

The priest, Henry Habib Ayrout, S.J., was known the length of the Egyptian Nile for his work with the poor and needy and among Middle East specialists for his definitive book on the *fellah*, the Egyptian peasant. [1] Upper class in background, charismatic in style and political in instinct, he became an indispensable guide for my exploration of the life, times and struggles of Egypt's Coptic Christians. He was connected to all parts of Egyptian society and he opened doors to every segment of the Coptic community. He had to remain anonymous while still alive, given the sensitive nature of the Coptic

question in Egypt. In this new edition of my book on the
Copts, credit can be given where it is due—to the irrepressible,
witty, outgoing cleric who was both intellectual and activist,
pious and political, sensitive and savvy. He knew all the key
sources and knew what was going on in Egypt, particularly
Christians faced.

The situation is not fundamentally different today for the
Copts. Different players, different incidents, different con-
frontations, but still a "lonely minority," still feeling the pressures of their life along the Nile. As a group, they personify
the struggle of any minority holding onto a strong identity
amidst religious, social, financial, and political pressures. Add
to that the historic problem of Egypt's Copts: living under the
threat of Moslem extremists who escalate militancy, into violence.

On one hand, there is the official government policy of a
Moslem/Coptic partnership and then there are the statistics
on Coptic exclusion from power in an authoritarian regime. In
particular, there are the periodic outbursts of violence on the
ground that remind the Copts that they are targets of extremists and that they remain vulnerable. After yet another out-
burst by Moslem militants who killed twenty-one Copts in a
single month, a bishop in southern Egypt, Anba Korolus,
described the persistent Coptic reaction toward the government's response to extremists. "Government policies toward
the Copts lead Moslems to believe that we are both insigni-
ficant and inconsequential. This encourages such attacks."

When the respected *Washington Post* correspondent, John
Lancaster, reported on Egypt's "Endangerered Christians"
in 1997, the Egyptian ambassador to the United States,
Ahmed Maher el Sayed, stated the government's unchanging
public and official position: "Christians in Egypt have always
enjoyed equal rights and privileges along with their Muslim
brethren and have occupied key posts in parliament, the
government and many international organizations."[2]

Back came the response by "an Egyptian Christian who grew up in Egypt and is very familiar with the current situation."[3] The particulars of his 1997 indictment are echoed by other members of the Coptic diaspora and confirmed by independent observers.

*Not a single Christian appointed to the judicial system for ten years.

* Presidential decrees required before Christians can build or repair their churches.

* Egypt's governing party (controlled by President Hosni Mubarak) did not nominate any Christians in the parliamentary elections. Mubarak subsequently appointed ten Christians to the parliament.

* Christians are excluded from the police academy and any military school.

* Christians must list their religion on ID cards and all job applications.

Sporadically, the Coptic situation gets attention. When Hilary Rodham Clinton met with President Mubarak on her visit to Egypt, she expressed concern about the treatment of Egypt's Copts—during a fifteen-minute courtesy call that stretched to an hour. While a U.S. State Department report on religious freedom in Egypt reported that for "the most part, members of the non-Muslim minorities worship without harassment," it pointed out that "Christians face discrimination based on tradition and some aspects of the law." The report also reported a frightening fact of life for the Copts: "Terrorists continue to attack churches and properties belonging to Christians and to target and kill Christian believers."[4] Meanwhile, members of the Coptic diaspora maintain a watch on what's happening to their brethren in Egypt, including an Internet presence (**http://www.copts.com**). They even have placed ads in the *Washington Post* during Congressional debates on religious persecution abroad.

But for the most part, Egyptian Copts remain largely invisible, "a lonely minority." What does it feel like—day in, day out—for Christian Copts to live in Moslem-dominated Egypt, to feel irrevocably Egyptian and to feel left out? What does their situation reveal about Egypt? How does it throw light on all minority situations? These are questions pursued in this book. Because the Coptic experience basically remains the same and the issues are as relevant as ever, this account of *A Lonely Minority* is being published again.

To get in touch with the realities of life in Egypt for the Copts, it was necessary to explore the nooks and crannies of Egyptian society and to draw on the hospitality, assistance and information provided by both Moslems and Christians. My sources were generous with their time and materials, including pamphlets, reports, documents, newspapers and books in French, English and Arabic that were available only in Egypt. The list of sources ranged from peasants in villages along the Nile to the privileged few (many of them Copts) in Cairo and Alexandria. It included social scientists, shopkeepers, schoolteachers, bishops, priests, monks, engineers, college students, government officials, judges, lawyers, doctors, one-time pashas and shopkeepers. Research involved trips throughout the countryside as well as discreet face-to-face meetings. One phrase still reverberates from my trips throughout Egypt with Father Ayrout. It was his reminder at each stop that it was time to get back into the car and move on. *En Voiture!*

After this book was published, Father Ayrout sent me a note in which he pointed out that the book "will have the effect of a bomb in certain circles." It did, and I subsequently learned that copies had to be smuggled into Egypt, sometimes by tearing out the pages and concealing them in the belongings of Copts flying home from trips abroad.

The Coptic issue remains sensitive and a parable of survival for a minority that is as much a part of Egypt as the life-giving Nile River. The scenario is universal. The controlling majority insists on dominating and maintaining control. A minority determined to keep its strong identity and to survive focuses on achievement and seeks full acceptance and a partnership role. An authoritarian government wants the issue to go away or at least stay out of sight. When the issue surfaces, it can have the "effect of a bomb."

The enduring topic sentence of this account is still the reminder of novelist Lawrence Durrell when he introduced Nessim, the exotic millionaire, in *Justine*, the first book in his Alexandria Quartet. "To begin with he was a Copt, not a Moslem."

1. Henry Habib Ayrout, S.J., *The Egyptian Peasant*, (Boston: Beacon Press, 1963). First published in France in 1938.
2. Letter to the *Washington Post* , April 11, 1997.
3. Response by Michael Meunier.
4. "Report on Religious Freedom in Egypt-State Department." July 22, 1997.

Part One:
The Coptic Presence

CHAPTER I
"True Egyptians"

A brief ride by horse and carriage across a modern Nile River bridge carries the occasional foreign visitor back and forth between Sohag, a provincial Egyptian city 333 miles south of Cairo, and the worn-out satellite town of Akhmim, which was once a grand ancient city of easy morals where, eventually, religious fanaticism led Christians to vandalize pagan temples and Moslems to murder Christians. Akhmim's remaining token of past glory is found in the products of hand looms that shuttle back and forth in the semi-darkness of mud huts. As if absorbing all the available light, Akhmim textiles emerge in a burst of color and design worthy of the town's ancient and renowned industry.

These Akhmim textiles symbolize the Coptic minority of Egypt. Spread across the plain wooden counters of local merchants, the colorful confusion and geometric patterns of the textiles conceal, at first, their identity. The men, women and children working in those mud huts have repeated endlessly in innumerable designs the self-imposed label of Egyptian Copts—the cross. Like the crosses in Akhmim textiles, the Copts are so thoroughly interwoven into the fabric of Egyptian society—geographically, sociologically and physically—

that they easily escape outside notice. Yet they probably number one in six Egyptians, which in an Egyptian population
of 24 million amounts to four million.

The modern-day Copts, who share with all minorities
their universal struggle to survive, are literally as old as the
Pharaohs and thus far as enduring as the Pyramids. Their
will to retain Coptic identity is endlessly repeated in their
history and in their contemporary situation. Symbolically,
all Egyptian Copts stand at the hand looms of Akhmim af-
firming that a collective will to survive has provided both
an ultimate basis and explanation for Coptic survival.

Viewed today from the West, the Copts are a major test
of modern coexistence between a large Christian minority
and a Moslem majority. In the Middle East, the Copts constitute the largest body of Christians in that part of the
world where Christianity was born. For Egypt, which is trying to mobilize all its human resources into a modern state,
the test may be decisive. For a mosaic of minorities in the
Middle Eastern countries of Syria, Jordan, Iraq, and Turkey,
the Coptic story can be read as handwriting on the wall. For
the Christians of Lebanon, who are maintaining an uneasy
dominance in a country evenly divided between Christians
and Moslems, their prospects in a Moslem Arab hegemony
can be deciphered from the Coptic situation in Egypt. It is a
problem echoed nearby in the tenuous Greek-Turkish partnership of Christian and Moslem in the island republic of
Cyprus. Involved, besides the Western values for which the
Copts stand, is the fate of tolerance and respect for the individual in the vast self-centered world community of 400
million Moslems. On an even larger stage, the Copts share
the drama of the world's minorities, ranging from the recent sufferings of Jews and Armenians to such current problems as Jews in Russia, Protestants in Spain.

As a minority, the Copts are unique. They are indigenous,
the original human material of the Nile Valley, and as they

are quick to point out, "Copt" is the Arabicized, then Euro-peanized, version of the Greek word for Egyptian. Indeed, it is likely that as much as 80 percent of Egypt's present Moslem population stems originally from Coptic stock, having been converted to Islam centuries ago. In the Coptic language, "Copts" means "people of Egypt" and the Copts use the term literally, referring to themselves as the "true Egyptians." Unlike the American Indians, the Copts have not practically disappeared under the sword of outsiders who conquered and settled; nor did they absorb and assimilate the invaders as did the Chinese. Unlike Armenians and Jews, the Copts have had little migration and no diaspora. It is both their burden and their fortune to have had only one home—the Nile Valley.

Christianity and the cross are well-suited to the Coptic mentality and to their experience as a conquered people or beleaguered minority. For any minority, its symbol is a badge in times of prosperity, a brand in times of trouble; the Coptic symbol of the cross always signifies suffering. Men and women wear crosses around their neck; in rural areas they tattoo it on the wrists of their children. Copts imbed designs showing the cross on the front of mud huts and stone houses. Priests make the sign of the cross thirty-six times on the bodies of baptized infants, signaling the uneasy lot of each newborn Copt and the protection of his group identity.

The Copts trace their Christianity back to St. Mark through an unbroken line of 116 Patriarchs or Egyptian popes and they cling to what they regard as "original Christianity," as the unchanged teachings of early Church fathers and councils. In the beginning, Christianity appealed to Egyptians as an outlet to resentment against foreign overlords who were the result of Greek and Roman conquest of Egypt. Christianity also appealed to them with its clear-cut morality and assurance of life after death, with which Egyptians have always been preoccupied.

While Christianity was a good fit in Egypt, it did not supersede the primary emphasis on Coptic identity; indeed, both church and cross have served the basic end of maintaining that identity. Placed in this light, creation of a national Egyptian church was inevitable for a people who have struggled continuously against outsiders. As far as the Copts are concerned, their historical experience with conquerors reaches back to Cambyses of Persia and to Alexander the Great, who delivered Egypt from Persian domination. It was one of many empty deliverances that the Copts have endured. Their historical experience has been a barometer of the rise and fall of empire and the ambitions of the strong and the mighty. Assyrians, Persians, Greeks, Romans, Arabs, Mamelukes, Turks, French, British and, lately, Moslem nationalists have held power in Egypt in an uninterrupted sequence, but not the Copts in their own land.

After the Council of Chalcedon in 451 A.D., the Copts built their church on a theological distinction that was more a surge of nationalism than a passion for theory. The Monophysite heresy which was condemned by the Council set the Egyptian church on its independent course. As Monophysites, the Copts believe that Jesus Christ was one person from two persons, God and man, and had one nature without "commingling" his human and divine natures, in contrast to the Roman Catholic dogma of one person with two natures. On all other dogmas, the Copts agree with the Greek Orthodox Church, but the Monophysite difference has been enough to set the Copts apart and there is little chance of their changing course in the foreseeable future.

Between the Council of Chalcedon, the crucial event for Copts as Christians, and the conquest of Egypt by the Arabs in 641, the crucial event for them as Egyptians, the national church took hold in Egypt, enlisting the overwhelming loyalty of the masses and generating strong leadership from militant monks. At the time of the Arab invasion, well over

90 percent of Egypt was Christian and for some centuries afterwards, though the Moslem garrisons ruled, the Christian faith prevailed.

When the Arab invaders arrived, two dominant traditions had emerged in Coptic Christianity—martyrdom and monasticism. Each still has its place in a contemporary description of the Copts. St. Anthony of Egypt, both the inspiration and technician of monasticism, had fathered the strongest monastic movement in Christendom. Egypt, during the middle of the fifth century, has been described as almost "one vast monastery." The tradition is still maintained that the Patriarch should be chosen from among the monks. Violation of the tradition in selecting the three Patriarchs prior to the present one is popularly blamed for the twentieth-century chaos which ensued in the church. Not only has the Patriarch been recruited from the monks, but also the bishops and his chief aides. The monks are the elite of the Coptic Church, custodians of power as well as symbols of sanctity.

The martyrs are the folk heroes of the Copts and their presence is imbedded in the Coptic calendar, which is dated from the year 284 A.D. in commemoration of the Era of Martyrs. In that year, the Roman emperor Diocletian began a reign marked by the blood of Christians. Between Diocletian's edict of persecution in 303 and his successor's edict of toleration in 311, an estimated 144,000 Egyptian Christians were slaughtered. Each September 11 when the Copts begin a new year of the martyrs, they invoke the martyrs' tradition, a reminder of a capacity and a readiness for ultimate defiance. It is an uneasy way to start a new year.

Under Arab rule, the Copts were gradually reduced from majority to minority, owing to migrations from Arabia and conversions to Islam. As cycles of toleration and persecution were set in motion by Arab rulers, many Copts converted to Islam under direct pressure or the indirect pressures of money-making opportunities and tax advantages. Though at the outset the Arab conquerors accorded certain rights to the Copts, the proselytizing vigor of Islam soon asserted itself. In the eighth century, Coptic monks were branded on the hand for taxation purposes. If a monk was caught un-branded, his hand was cut off. Meanwhile, heavy taxes were imposed on the Copts in lieu of the military service from which they were excluded. In the ninth century, the Coptic peasantry and the Arabs began to intermingle as conversions to Islam increased and Arabic began displacing the Coptic language, which had come into being between 250 and 350. The Coptic language, which began as vernacular Egyptian written in Greek letters, was by the tenth century practically relegated to the observance of religious liturgy. This can be regarded as reflecting the Copts' shift from a numerical majority to a numerical minority.

With the exception of the reign of the insane Caliph al-Hakim (996-1021), the Fatimid period in Egypt from 969 to 1171, was marked by relative tolerance. But with the rise of the Mameluke Dynasty of slaves and soldiers from 1250 until the Turkish conquest in 1517, the Copts once again ex-perienced direct and sometimes bloody persecution. Possibly the lowest point in relations between Copts and Moslems was reached in 1320 when fanatical Moslems destroyed and looted all the principal churches of Egypt. The Copts re-taliated by burning many mosques, palaces, and private houses. The final blow was struck when the Sultan per-mitted a massacre of Christians. A special turban was made mandatory for Christians, a bell had to be worn by Christians using the public bath, and Christians could not ride horses, mules or even asses unless they sat facing backward. Copts were expelled from all public offices and from the employ of Moslem dignitaries. It was a time of mass conversions.

When the Ottoman Turks conquered Egypt in 1517, the Coptic-Moslem relationship was well established; it was a suspicious and uneasy truce frequently interrupted by violence. The Ottoman Empire, in establishing a horizontal system of administrative units called millets, laid the groundwork for the present formal structure of the Coptic community. The millets were organized along religious lines under the direction of an ecclesiastical dignitary who had power over civil as well as religious matters. The head of the millet was responsible for registration of births, marriages, deaths and wills, maintenance of civil law courts, and raising of taxes. The contemporary Community Council of the Copts is heir to the millet of the Ottoman Empire. The Council is a functioning apparatus which organizes the Copts into a community whose members are taken in at birth and remain members until death. The community's base is religious, but its membership is automatic and hereditary. An Egyptian remains a Copt, even if he stops believing in God, for the line between community and church is still not drawn clearly in Egypt or anywhere else in the Middle East.

The short-lived occupation of Egypt (1798-1801) by Napoleon shattered the illusion of invincibility that the self-centered world of Islam had nurtured, and it introduced Western influences to which the Arab world is still adjusting. While the Copts felt that the French were indifferent to their situation in Egypt, the Moslems accused the Copts of cooperating with the foreigner. Both the Coptic complaint and the Moslem accusation foreshadowed similar attitudes that arose during the British occupation of Egypt from 1882 to 1922.

In the wake of the French departure, Mohammed Ali, a dynamic and ruthless Albanian mercenary who had been in the military service of the Ottomans, seized control of Egypt. His policy of selecting the best men for government positions without regard to religion opened the way for Copts to reach high positions. He was the first ruler in modern Egyptian history to raise Coptic functionaries to the honorary

title of bey and to surround himself with Christian aides.
Moreover, he abrogated all repressive laws against Christians
and suppressed any outbreaks of fanaticism. Mohammed Ali
was not a liberal but a ruler with a strong secular bent and
a modern style of stressing effective government.

Under his son, Said, the army was opened up to the Copts,
and for the first time since the Arab conquest, Copts were
permitted to bear arms. Since the suppression of the last great
Coptic revolt in the ninth century it had been almost impossible for a Copt to obtain any arms. When the religious
bar was removed and Copts were conscripted into the army,
the decree was misused as an instrument of persecution, both
in the wholesale conscripting of Coptic males and the harsh
treatment they received. The decree was rescinded after the
Coptic Patriarch put pressure on Said through influential
Englishmen. Said's successor, Ismail, the first ruler to aid
Coptic schools, stressed the notion that the category Egyptian
had nothing to do with religion and he even put Copts into
his consultative assembly and into the courts.

Thus, the rise of Mohammed Ali in the early nineteenth
century marked a turn for the better for the Copts and set
the stage for the contemporary chapter in the history of the
"true Egyptians." The Copts emerge as a group with a multiple identity—as a church, a community, a nation, a beleaguered minority. Also add a privileged few, for under
the pressure of minority status and cycles of persecution,
discrimination and toleration, the Copts sought protection
in money and skills. As they were transformed from majority to minority after the Arab invasion, the Copts became
the artisans, physicians and clerks of Egypt as well as the
money lenders, tax collectors and financiers. They developed
highly-valued skills in business, commerce and the professions; the hand at the accountant's ledger, the engineer's
drawing board, the pharmacist's pestle and the surgeon's
table was Coptic. Moslems dominated politics and govern-

ment, but the Copts often handled the money and later acquired land. While Moslems despised Copts, foreign interests with heavy investments in Egypt valued them as competent and trustworthy and appreciated their knowledge of French and English. By any yardstick, the proportion of Copts among the rich, the educated, and the skilled in Egypt far surpassed their numbers.

Out of their composite identity as a church, community, potential nation, beleaguered minority and privileged few arises the two-sided paradox of the modern Copts. There are many reasons why they should constitute a major force in the current movement to create a New Egypt, living up to the nineteenth century prophecy quoted by Lord Cromer in 1908 in his book *Modern Egypt:* "The Copts will probably occupy no small part of the field in the future history of Egypt." They should be strong, but actually they are weak, which is one side of the paradox. On the other hand, the Coptic decline since the Arab invasion conceivably should have led by now to loss of identity and disappearance from the Nile Valley. Instead, there are now phoenix-like signs of a Coptic resurgence—the other side of the paradox.

The potential power of the Copts is evident in their involvement with all aspects of Egyptian life as well as their strong motivation to earn and learn. The intellectual aptitudes of the Copts, their higher per capita income and their cultural strength are not limited to an urban ghetto, but reproduced up and down the social levels throughout the country.

The Coptic assets are re-enforced by an intense family life and a highly emotional attachment to their religion. A Catholic priest who works closely with the Copts illustrated their religious feelings by describing what happened when a Cairo cinema showed a tired Hollywood film on the life of Christ. The Copts jammed the cinema for showing after showing, and became so involved in the movie—shouting, sighing and weeping—that they turned the "cinema into a house of worship." In Upper Egypt, a missionary nun said that Coptic women "burst into tears" when told about their sins. In the individual family unit, the tools of survival have been forged under the pressure of a dual responsibility to compete and succeed for the sake of family honor and to cooperate in helping members of the family. By extension, this duty reaches out to all members of church and community.

Presumably this group arsenal would assure the Copts a major position of power. Native to the country and an integral part of the sanctified nationalist movement that fought the British, the Copts have a natural role to play in Egyptian dreams of glory. They are so many with so much to contribute. Yet, a feeling of helplessness is overwhelming the Copts; most feel they are legitimate heirs to the land of Egypt who are deprived of their inheritance.

At the same time, the very persistence of the modern Copts defies all the forces that have been pushing them downhill to oblivion. Turned inward by a hostile environment, the Copts have looked to themselves in recent times and found a church whose clergy has been, in the main, either corrupt or ignorant. On one count or the other, priests and bishops lost any claim to leadership. In monasteries, which once inspired all Christendom, monks idled away the years, neither in spirituality nor learning.

The Coptic religion has been diluted by heavy doses of superstition and commercialism, especially at rural religious festivals, while the intellectual content remained primitive. When the librarian at the Patriarchate was asked about church theologians, he replied, before correcting himself on second thought: "We had one, but he died." By default, the content of Coptic life has become part Pharaonic, part Christian, part Oriental, part petit bourgeois.

Meanwhile, the rewards of conversion to Islam reached

out in such advantages as easy divorce and remarriage, social acceptance as part of the dominant Moslem community, and a favored position under the law. While other Middle Eastern minorities were propped up by foreign interests, the Copts were left on their own. They rejected affiliation with foreign Protestantism and Roman Catholicism and then proceeded to devour each other with internal rivalries within the laity and between laity and hierarchy.

Surprisingly, examination of the Copts at mid-century gives evidence of a renaissance from Alexandria on the Mediterranean to the hinterland of Upper Egypt. Christian missionaries, who traditionally focus on the Copts, report that new life is stirring. A rising generation of priests and monks, many of them recruited from the professional classes, has become influential. The Patriarch chosen in 1959 is imposing strict controls over the churches; life in the monasteries is once again pointed in the direction of Antonian ideals. A handful of families even is resurrecting the dead Coptic language. At Cairo's rejuvenated Institute of Coptic Studies, a cultural and intellectual framework for the Coptic identity is being provided for both laity and clergy.

From a purely spiritual point of view, the future of the Copts can be said to rest with God. As an Egyptian Jesuit said: "If it is God's will that the Coptic Church survive, then it will." Though this may constitute an ultimate answer, the particular Jesuit, as well as the rest of Christian Egypt, is concerned about the worldly response the modern Copts must make to meet the future. The response must come from them, but not without involving the Moslem majority and the sum total of their own identity.

CHAPTER II
Political Partners

The contemporary mood of the Copts is influenced by the eventual failure of a precarious political marriage with the Moslems. Since their courtship was motivated by common opposition to the British, rather than mutual attraction, the union suffered from the departure of the object of mutual animosity. The British ended in 1922 the occupation they began in 1882, but not until Moslems and Copts had joined hands in the Egyptian nationalist movement and in the Wafd, the country's dominant political party after independence. Though the union had its ups and downs, it lasted until 1942, when it broke up in a public quarrel between the leading Copt and the leading Moslem in the Wafd Party.

In the beginning, the Copts were well disposed to the British, who occupied Egypt in the wake of financial chaos brought on by heavy expenditures for foreign adventures and public works, not the least of which was the Suez Canal (opened in 1869). The prophetic circumstances foreshadowed, in many ways, Britain's unsuccessful Suez adventure in the middle of the following century. Britain sent troops against a military strong man, Arabi Pasha, who had risen from humble origins to become the figurehead of a revolu-

14

tionary movement. Arabi also had unnerved the Copts by proclaiming that Islam was endangered by Christians being placed in authority. France, which had been directing Egyptian internal reform along with Britain in order to protect their heavy financial interests, refused to join the invasion. On September 13, 1882, when Arabi was defeated in the battle of Tel el-Kebir, the British went it alone in Egypt.

Before long, the Copts felt spurned by their British deliverers, who in turn were shocked at what they considered the Coptic demand for special treatment. The British sense of justice was offended. No one can summarize the reaction with more authority or authenticity than the redoubtable Lord Cromer, Britain's de facto ruler of Egypt from 1883 to 1907: "The principles of strict impartiality on which the Englishman proceeded were foreign to the nature of the Copt . . . He thought that the Englishman's justice to the Moslem involved injustice to himself, for he was apt, perhaps unconsciously, to hold that injustice and absence of favoritism to Copts were well-nigh synonymous terms."

In order to present their side of the argument, the Copts sent a journalist to England a few years before World War I. In a slender volume, *Copts and Moslems under British Control* (1911), which occupies a special place in the history of the Coptic question, Kyriakos Mikhail answered Cromer: "We [Copts] have never asked for any favor at the hands of the government. We have asked for justice and equality with Egyptians, and for a full participation in the fruits which have resulted from the new regime." The burden of the charge was that—irony of ironies—the Coptic position in Egypt had deteriorated though the country was occupied by fellow Christians! But it should be noted that Mohammed Ali and his successors could—as Moslems—make concessions to the Copts without being open to the charge that they were favoring their own kind.

The British regarded themselves as custodians rather than

conquerors; they tended to manipulate rather than dictate. Taking seriously their burden of keeping the "natives" quiet, the British had to consider the attitude of the Moslems, the third and majority party in the situation. While the Moslems might tolerate the Copts, they were by no means ready to love them and certainly not to take orders from them. Lord Cromer's successor, Sir Eldon Gorst, sounded the warning: "In Upper Egypt at the present time [1911] the Copt is prosperous but not popular. Were he to be placed in a high executive post, in addition to his lack of natural aptitude for it, he would find a majority of the population animated by antagonistic feelings toward him, and he could not count on ready obedience and cooperation".

Meeting in the main Coptic city of Assyut in March 1911, the Copts held a controversial congress that set down five major grievances that are a landmark in their demands for equality. Although they appeared in Kyriakos Mikhail's book in 1911, they sound current enough to repeat:

1. As a Christian body of people, the Copts are forced to violate the commandments of their religion by Sunday labor.
2. A large number of administrative posts in the government service are entirely closed to Copts, and it is felt that in general they are not promoted in accordance with their capabilities and merit.
3. Under the existing electoral system in Egypt they are left unrepresented on the Provincial Councils.
4. The Copts have no equal right to take advantage of the educational facilities provided by the new Provincial Councils.
5. The Copts claim that government grants should be bestowed on deserving institutions without invidious distinction of race or creed.

Meanwhile, Moslem nationalist leaders held out their arms to the Copts. Under the influence of French liberalism, Egyptian nationalism was being defined without a religious base by Mustafa Kamel, early in this century, and later by Saad Zaghlul, the statesman-like figure who dominated the

Egyptian independence movement. Nationalist demonstrators marched behind banners displaying the cross and crescent and in the final phases of resistance to the British from 1919 to 1921, Moslem-Coptic rapprochement was greater than it has been before or after. Relations were not even upset when a prominent Copt violated the political boycott organized by the nationalists against the British. In fact, when Yusef Wahba cooperated with the British by forming a cabinet, a fellow Copt tried to assassinate him.

After independence, Zaghlul acted on his public statements concerning the place of the Copts: "Egypt belongs to Copts as well as Moslems. All have a right to the same freedom and the same privileges." The cabinet he formed in 1926 placed two Copts in positions second only to his. Makram Ebeid Pasha became finance minister and Wasif Butros Ghali became foreign minister. After Zaghlul's death in 1927, the Wafd leadership fell to Nahas Pasha, who dominated the party in conjunction with Makram Ebeid Pasha, who might have become a prime minister if he hadn't been a Copt.

The Moslem-Coptic union in the Wafd was continuously imperiled by the latent antagonism of the masses, which its political opponents were always ready to exploit. Even while Zaghlul was alive, the 1926 cabinet containing two Copts aroused the political charge that "this delegation of fanatical Copts" was trying to "establish their supremacy over the Moslems." Then in the 1940's, Nahas Pasha the Moslem and Makram Ebeid Pasha the Copt split and most of the Copts left the Wafd.

Moslem and Coptic leadership, however enlightened, had to cope with popular stereotypes that poisoned relations between the two groups and still retain their influence. As with all stereotypes there are enough scraps of truth to sustain the distortions. Copts regard Moslems as children of fanaticism and fathers of violence, as unintelligent and un-

reliable, lacking in moral standards or a sense of responsibility and loyalty. Moslems see Copts as children of
craftiness and fathers of criticism, shrewd, clannish and ready
to do business with foreigners. They see the Copts as money
changers, artisans and clerks, as people for hire and as men
without courage (though historically the Moslems prevented
the Copts from bearing arms). It is the cleavage between
those with power and those with skill, the tradition of the
conqueror and of the subjugated, a tale of the hound and
the hare.

Fundamentally, it is the figure of Mohammed that stands
between the two groups and the difference can be stated
simply: Mohammed is the central historical and religious
fact for Moslems; Christianity rejects him. Moslems regard
Christianity as an inferior religion whose divine revelation
has stopped at Christ, regarded by Moslems as a prophet who
was surpassed by the last and greatest prophet. The Islamic
belief that it possesses the final and perfect form of divine
revelation has more than religious significance, for Mohammed was both a political and religious visionary who did not
separate church and state. Islam has never been concerned
with rendering unto Caesar, for it admits of no separation
of the secular and the religious. The Moslem religion is supreme and so is its community, thereby placing all other
religious communities in an inferior position. For the orthodox Moslem as well as for the masses it is inconceivable that
a Copt (or anyone else from an inferior community) should
have authority over Moslems. Wilfred Cantwell Smith, a
leading contemporary scholar of Islam, points up, in his
Islam in Modern History (1959), the tenuous position of
minorities in Islam: "Nowhere in the Moslem world (except
perhaps in Indonesia) do Moslems feel that a non-Moslem is
'one of us.' And nowhere do the minorities feel accepted."

In the years preceding the rise of the Nasser regime, the
Copts were publishing their complaints, though sometimes

secretly as in the case of a highly-charged book titled *Far-riq Tasud* [*Divide and Conquer*]. The tone of the book and the feelings surrounding it in 1950 are epitomized in the introduction written by the late Salama Mousa, a Copt and one of the leading figures in contemporary Arabic literature.

It is my belief that when our Moslem brothers read this book and note the complaints of the Copts, they will rise to help them achieve justice . . . I feel certain that everyone who reads this book will feel personally responsible for the fate of the Copts and will feel that he must raise his voice and make all the world understand the necessity of quickly doing justice to the Copts—before extreme bitterness takes hold of the Copts and outweighs their national spirit. In that way lies destruction for all.

Unity between the Moslem and the Copt was the symbol of the 1919 revolution, and we used to cry out: "Long live the Crescent and the Cross." I heard learned men from al-Azhar [the Islamic university] speaking in the churches and I saw and heard priests greeted by al-Azhar. This unity should have been with us today, but new developments deflected the tide of our history. It is the mission of the author of *Farriq Tasud* to warn us of these changes and the dangers to Egypt in them.

In the last years of King Farouk's reign, impassioned complaints were published in the Coptic daily, "Misr," and the outspoken weekly, "Al-Manarat." A selection of the articles was published in pamphlet form under the title "The Cry of Egypt's Copts," by an interested group in New York. Statements such as these were quoted in the 1951 pamphlet:

But now, in this twentieth century, people are forging chains and irons to limit the freedom of worship of the Christians and deprive them even of the liberty to build churches. [Feb. 17, 1951, "Misr."] The Wafd seems to have forgotten that there are Copts qualified for nomination [to the Egyptian Senate] and that this nation and people are composed of two elements, Moslem and Copt . . . three million Copts did not pass by the lists in silence and quiet. No, on their lips was a bitter smile, remembering with pain a past happy era when the Wafd had many Coptic members, deputies and senators. May God have mercy on that time and on Saad Zaghlul. (March 23, 1951, "Misr.")

The bitterest articles were published in "Al-Manarat," whose editor and publisher, Abuna (Father) Sergius, was a dynamic Coptic priest who captured the imagination of Egyptians early in the independence movement. He mounted the pulpit in al-Azhar Mosque, the citadel of orthodox Islam, three times daily during one phase of the Egyptian agitation for independence after World War I. His sermon: freedom for all Egyptians. On February 19, 1951, he wrote in his weekly:

Were the people of [ancient] Israel more miserable then in Egypt than the sons of the Copts are now? When the sons of Israel were thrown out of Egypt and crossed the Red Sea, they found a desert to take refuge in. But for the Copts, still pursued and persecuted by their countrymen, what escape is there, what deserts will give them refuge?

The aged priest Sergius and the old politician Makram Ebeid personify the Coptic experience in this century and within the Coptic context they stand out as epic figures, the one a leader of men, the other a disappointed nationalist with strong commitments and violent reactions. In the month of June 1961, the old politician died in obscurity, his life's work undone; the priest lived on, his untamed spirit trapped in an enfeebled body. His weekly journal had been suppressed in the early years of the Nasser regime and his voice could no longer be heard sounding the alarm for the Copts. In fact, no voice of complaint could be heard; it was not permitted by the Nasser regime.

CHAPTER III

The "Best Egyptians"

Generally speaking, the Copts regard themselves as the most
intelligent, most loyal, most law-abiding, and worthiest citizens of Egypt. As a matron from Assyut said while sum-
mering in Alexandria, "We feel we are tops," and since she
is a Copt the "we" meant not Egyptians in general, but
Copts in particular.

The Copts point out that their people rarely beg or steal,
that their daughters refuse to work as servants and almost
never end up as ladies of the night, that their children are
the best behaved, their family life is exemplary and their
standards are the highest in the country.

This is the Coptic self-image, and under the pressure of
minority status and Christian values, it comes close to reality,
judging from personal investigation and the testimony of the
knowledgeable and the reliable. Although the regime dis-
courages comparisons on a religious basis and hampers in-
formation-gathering along these lines, it was possible to
examine the Coptic self-image in the cold light of numbers
(bearing in mind that Copts may comprise as much as 16
percent of the total population and that the category Christians embraces slightly more than the Copts).

21

At the extremes of anti-social behavior, the government's private tally on the religious background of newly admitted prisoners is a persuasive indicator. The figures cover those Egyptians entering prison in 1958 and 1959 after conviction. Combining murder, intent to murder and serious assaults, Moslems outnumbered Christians 1,612 to 73, and 1,709 to 57 in 1958 and 1959, respectively. In the category of thefts, it was 11,000 Moslems to 354 Christians in 1958 and 9,243 to 261 in 1959. For violation of duties as court-appointed trustees, 3,106 Moslems went to prison in 1958, compared to 110 Christians, 3,230 to 82 in 1959.

The Copts also have a remarkably clean record in the marginal areas of lawbreaking that reflect a loss of self-respect. Prison statistics show a preponderance of new Moslem prisoners over Christians—703 to 12 and 596 to 16—for sale of drugs, and 1,919 to 42 and 2,520 to 62 for use of drugs in 1958 and 1959 respectively. There were 6,978 Moslems imprisoned in 1958 for begging, compared to 237 Christians, 6,218 to 204 in 1959.

Coptic prostitutes are practically unheard of in Egypt, as is illustrated by a story (told of course by Copts) of the young woman who petitioned the court to change her religion from Coptic to Moslem. In the course of the proceedings, the judge asked why she wanted to change her religion. Was it for love, a change of faith, the inspiration of the Koran, the failure of Christianity? The young woman replied: "How can I remain a Copt and be a prostitute?" When Egypt's National Center for Social and Criminological Research studied 10,003 women arrested for prostitution in Cairo over a twelve-month period beginning October 18, 1957, it found that 98.1 percent of the prostitutes were Moslems.

The Copts are particularly proud of their family life, the closeness of parent-child relationships and the rarity of divorce. In comparison with Moslems, who can divorce their wives merely by registering the end of the marriage, the

Copts have the Christian abhorrence of divorce, though it is possible to get a divorce on certain grounds. Figures obtained from the Egyptian Ministry of Justice showed that in the three years 1956 to 1958 there was one Moslem divorce for every three Moslem marriages.

An active Coptic parishioner described the differing contexts of family life. In the Coptic community, where marriage is taken for granted as a permanent institution, the child has a sense of security and usually a close relationship with both parents. Among Moslems, for whom divorce is both a real and a psychological threat, children are often reared by aunts, uncles or other members of the family; generally there is less emphasis on intimate relationship between the child and both parents, especially during adolescence. In a 1960 report on juvenile delinquency, Egypt's Social Research Center found that over a 15-month period 94 percent of the juveniles arrested were Moslems.

As to their loyalty to Egypt, many Copts complain that Nasser doesn't realize how much he can rely upon them, that he should trust them rather than the many "opportunists" who surround him. At each new roundup of spies, the Copts examine the names carefully to make sure that none of the spies is one of them. A member of the landowning Coptic aristocracy recalled her apprehension after a spy roundup when she was in doubt about one of the names and her relief upon learning that he was not a Copt. She also complained about Lawrence Durrell's Alexandria Quartet, which involved the Copts in a conspiracy with Zionists against the Egyptian government. Durrell has been quoted as saying: "I dreamed up for the story a conspiracy of the Copts against the Egyptians. It never existed, except in my imagination. I asked an expert to read what I had written and he was worried that the Egyptians would actually punish the Copts *now* for this nonexistent conspiracy."

Coptic sensitivity extends to the question of how many

Copts there really are in Egypt and it is here that a weary traveler enters the labyrinthine ways of Middle Eastern statistics, which Egyptian social scientists properly characterize as "the dark numbers." Estimates are tossed back and forth the way a rug is bought in Cairo bazaars, with many Copts overestimating their numbers at five, six, seven millions and insisting that one in five or one in four Egyptians is a Copt. The government, in turn, underestimates their numbers, which Copts regard as an attempt to undermine their claims by miscounting. The fewer Copts that are counted the more justification for government indifference toward them.

In the spring of 1960, a stir was caused among the Copts by a pre-census interview with the head of the governmental statistical department published in the popular French-language magazine "Images." The editor, a Christian, was regarded as a "traitor" merely for publishing the statements made by the Moslem official, who, incidentally, is married to a Christian. According to this man who was about to direct the national census, the Christians comprise only 7.6 percent of the Egyptian population with both Moslems and Copts increasing at the same rate. To the Copts, and many others, this sounded like an announcement of how the census would turn out. Barring government juggling of the census—not inconceivable in the Middle East—there is no doubt that head-counting in Egypt is an erratic operation hampered by all the problems of underdeveloped countries with a tradition of suspicion, especially by the minority, toward the census taker.

The best solution was to turn from Copts and Moslems to Protestant and Catholic sources in Egypt and abroad. Since Christianity in Egypt is their business and the Copts their raw material, they have carefully estimated the actual number of Copts. Their composite verdict is an estimate of close to four million Copts, about a million more than the government estimate for a population of 24 million. The accuracy of the estimate of four million Copts was supported by the belated results of the 1960 Egyptian census. On May 20, 1962, the New York "Times" Cairo correspondent, Jay Walz, cited census figures showing 27 million Egyptians and reported that the total included four million Copts. This represents a population 14.8 percent Coptic, close to the 16 percent estimate and much higher than ever officially reported heretofore. Meanwhile, the Nasser regime has prevented the Coptic Church from conducting a church census of its own.

The Copts are so jealous of their identity that many resent being labelled as Christians on their Egyptian identity cards. It isn't the religious labelling that annoys them, but the lumping together with the other Christians who carry a foreign connotation and, often, a foreign passport. These other Christians in Egypt included about 100,000 Catholic Copts affiliated with Rome, as are a mosaic of other Catholics in the Latin rite and in the various Oriental rites: Melkites, Maronites, Armenians, Syrians and Chaldeans. Non-Catholic Christians include the Greek Orthodox, Armenians, Jacobites and Protestants, the latter estimated at 100,000. The Christians have been reduced in number by the continuous exodus of foreigners from Egypt since the 1956 attack on Suez by Israel, France and England. The Copts, who remain in Egypt as they always have, want to stress their identity as Egyptians and to them this means bearing the label Copt.

For the Copts, rejection has moved in both directions. While they did not feel fully accepted by Westerners, the Copts also discouraged collaboration with other Christian groups, though the latter offered the possibility of Western sympathy and support. The Copts were too jealous of their independence as Christians and their identity as Egyptians. The Copts feared the Moslems and often pursued their friendship. At the same time, the Copts felt superior to them and tended to remain aloof.

Even Copts who join other Christian churches retain an ambiguous allegiance to their original identity that confounds any Western missionary in search of total conversion. One of the most prominent Catholic Coptic women in Egypt described the situation in her family: "My mother is a Catholic Copt and my father Orthodox Egyptian Copt. My father said it is all right to follow the Catholic Church but you must be baptized Orthodox, marry Orthodox and die in the Orthodox Church. My own daughter when she marries will marry in the Orthodox Church." The wife of a leading YMCA executive explained that her family, originally from Upper Egypt, was converted to Protestantism about 50 years ago. "But we are still Copts. We go to the Coptic church on the big holidays, Easter, Christmas. Many of my cousins are converted to Protestantism. There must be a hundred or a hundred and fifty living in Heliopolis [a Cairo suburb]. But they will have their children married in the Coptic Church." In such ways, the Copts demonstrate their dependence on the Church of Egypt to sanction their activities and reaffirm their Coptic identity.

The Copts stress competition and achievement, and in the vicious circle of majority-minority tensions greater Moslem rejection has intensified Coptic competitiveness, which in turn provokes greater aggressiveness on the part of the Moslems. The conflict stems partly from the differing orientations of the Moslem and Coptic communities. The Moslem inclination is toward assured status and preference based on membership in the majority religion, while the Copts stress a race in which the best man wins. And they do not hesitate to tell you that the best man always turns out to be a Copt.

The case of a Coptic engineer working for the government illustrates the differing orientations. The engineer waited five years for promotion while a total of 17 engineers, less qualified Moslems in lower ranks, were promoted over him. In the end he had a nervous breakdown, resigned, and eventually found a job with a private firm (a better job). One of the Moslem engineers promoted over him had at one point tried to console him by offering an explanation of why he was passed over. "Look at me. I have very little," he said. "You have a house in Zamalek, a wife, children that you send to a good school. You even take a vacation in Europe every few years. You have some money from your father that helps you. I do not even have a grapevine to my name. Don't you think that counts too?" But not a word about ability and qualifications.

When an army officer close to the regime was chided good-naturedly by a priest about the exclusion of Copts from top government positions, he replied half in jest: "Don't be angry with us, Father. You know we are stupid, idle people. Meanwhile, the Copts are growing quickly. We must keep them down or we will be swallowed by them."

In Egyptian colleges and universities, Coptic students excel, for they place a premium on education and feel they must make up for the preference accorded Moslems. In the late 1940's, the proportion of Copts in Egyptian schools above the elementary level reached one in four. Coptic students are convinced that grades and class standing are manipulated in favor of the Moslems. A young Copt, who recently graduated from Cairo University and whose father is on the faculty, summed up the attitude. "At the university, it was taken for granted that grades are adjusted in favor of the Moslem students, especially in the last year, since your class ranking when you graduate counts for life. The Moslems are as intelligent as the Copts, but the latter work harder because they need higher grades to get a chance."

Since the careers chosen by outstanding Copts have always followed the path of most opportunity, there have been distinct trends beginning with the grandfathers and great

grandfathers of today's university students. Combining trade
and agriculture, the most successful Copts in the last century
established a land-owning aristocracy. Their sons made repu-
tations in the professions of law and medicine, with the
lawyers gravitating into politics. As law and medicine became crowded, engineering, pharmacy and accounting became popular. During the 1940's, Copts became middlemen,
entering the business of contracting or export-import. In
recent years, some Copts from the leading families have gone
full cycle, becoming tradesmen, but on the level of the high-
fashion couturier shop in Cairo's new Hilton Hotel. The
army, the new source of Egyptian elite, has always been
regarded as Moslem territory and for the Copts it has never
been a high-prestige vocation.

The pragmatic, rather than the intellectual, appeals to the
Copts, for while they are characterized by intelligence, they
are deficient in scholarly output or cultural activity. The
absence, for instance, of a literary tradition is noteworthy.
Though the Coptic situation is grist for the novelist, poet
or social critic, it has mainly fed the polemicist. Coptic
scholarship tends to be self-centered and chauvinistic, too
often uncritical, and usually focused on their ancient Egyptian or early Coptic heritage. For a historical description of
their past, modern Copts depend on a sympathetic two-
volume work, *The Story of the Church of Egypt*, which
was published in 1897 and sells at a premium in Cairo book-
stores when copies can be obtained. Its author, Mrs. E. L.
Butcher, was English.

In the cities, Copts are found on all social and economic
levels, though their self-image is located in the middle class.
The city of Alexandria typifies both reality and image. In
contrast to the Coptic version of 200,000 in Alexandria's
population of 1.5 million, the total was estimated at 132,000
by a well-informed Franciscan missionary who has methodi-
cally studied the city's Coptic community. He reported

that about half are impoverished slum-dwellers located along the Mahmoudieh Canal where they squatted after migrating from Upper Egypt. Comparatively recent arrivals, they are rural poor transferred to the city and clustered in population units of 30,000, 22,000 and 10,000. They work as laborers and peddlers, retaining marginal Coptic identity as they scratch out an existence, neglected by a lax clergy and ignored by most of their better-established co-religionists.

Those Copts who meet the income requirements for voting in Coptic Community Council elections comprise a middle class that earns about seven times the three or four pounds earned monthly by the lower class. The rolls of eligible voters included the names of 1,600 Copts who are regarded as the leading members of the Alexandria community. This group is composed of university professors, doctors, lawyers, wealthy businessmen and high-ranking government employees. The 1,600 comprise the mailing list for invitations to major church functions.

The heart of the middle class is government employees, many of them in customs and railway services, shopkeepers, and skilled craftsmen. Below them are factory workers, waiters and trolley conductors. According to the head of Alexandria's Community Council, even Copts with small incomes and low social standing are a proud lot with organizations of their own. He cited a recent appearance by the head of one such organization, a trolley conductor, who challenged the policy of the Community Council. "The lowest Copt," he said, "considers himself as good as anyone and is not afraid to speak his mind."

At the top of the Alexandria community are the rich land-owning Coptic families, who have been hit hard by Egyptian land reform though enough remains to recall their past luxury. One elite family, for instance, retains its magnificent Mediterranean villa which was once manned by twenty-four servants. To maintain the establishment, the

number of servants has been reduced and two sons, along
with their families, have moved in, contributing to the up-
keep. Still, each member of the family has his own car and
though the villa's grand lady is reduced to a Fiat Millecento
she has a chauffeur. Still echoing through the drawing room
as the servants serve refreshments are the sounds of the pasha
class of Egypt: Jews, Christians and Moslems talking the
common language of wealth and privilege and, as ever, lacking social responsibility. Yet in their decline, the Coptic elite
families have left a valuable bequest: their middle-aged sons
are among the country's leading doctors, scientists, lawyers,
architects, engineers, bankers and businessmen.

Along with the other Christians, the Copts have been the
main transmitters of Western and modern attitudes in Egypt.
The Coptic elite and upper middle class sent their sons
abroad to study, while their daughters were the leading examples of increasing female emancipation at home. As the
most receptive pupils of Western ways, Copts became the
first (and almost the only) converts to Western Christianity,
a large part of the student body in Western-operated schools,
enthusiastic devotees of Western clothes, décor and styles.
But the Copts never discarded their traditionalism, and
nowhere is this more evident than in their deep visceral
attachment to the land of the Nile.

Their characteristic rootedness as Egyptians, commonly
explained as the result of centuries as a farming people
clinging to the banks of the Nile, is reflected in sights, sounds
and atmosphere that are meaningful to all Egyptians.

Dominating the intangible pull of Egypt is the ever present Nile, which is more than a constant backdrop. Its varying colors and changing water levels signal the coming and
going of the Nile flood that sets the rhythm of farming in a
rainless country and holds the attention of all Egyptians. No
Egyptian is ever far from his river and, except for the Alex-
andrines whose personality is split by looking outward to-

ward the Mediterranean, the Egyptians are a hinterland people with little appetite for travel, even inside their own country. They glorify their national dishes, including the variety of concoctions surrounding the simple bean. The exasperating malaise that afflicts life in Egypt becomes a mildly-attractive addiction. Most of all, they have a sense of all-encompassing familiarity at home and a sense of alienation when abroad. Even the sound of Arabic in a faraway place evokes an enthusiastic response. Foreigners who have lived in Egypt confirm the compelling attraction of the country by acknowledging the validity of the adage that once having drunk the waters of the Nile, you are bound to return someday. There is something particularly excruciating about Egyptian nostalgia for Egypt; it is sometimes outlandish, but the attachment flows through all Egyptians, as the Nile through Egypt.

In their historical refusal to emigrate, or even to enlist outside aid, the Copts have placed a geographic boundary (the banks of the Nile) on their critical test of Moslem-Christian relations. The problem and, also, the challenge to the Egyptian government is inescapable because of the commitment to remain—as Copts—and work out their future in the place where they have always been. This persistence, above all, dominates the Copts' self-image and is the strongest psychological proof that they are, indeed, "true Egyptians."

CHAPTER IV

A New Year, an Old Story

The New Year 1677, according to the Coptic martyrs' calendar, was launched September 10, 1960, in the courtyard of al-Tewfik Coptic school in Cairo's Faggalah section. Schoolchildren performed one-act plays, young men played Coptic music, Coptic dignitaries recalled the martyrs, an army general represented President Nasser and an archbishop represented the Patriarch, Anba Kirillus VI. The melody of Coptic glory was counterpointed by proclamations of Coptic-Moslem brotherhood under the leadership of Nasser. On view was the public Copt.

Conspicuous in the second row of the audience was a spirited Coptic priest who a few days before had poured tea and offered chocolate sweets from Groppi's as he talked bitterly in his home of the weakness of church leadership and the antagonism of the regime. A Coptic journalist from a mass circulation Cairo daily, who waved to his many friends and nodded respectfully to the clergy, had talked in private of government hostility and clerical corruption. A mutual friend had to dissuade him from running to the secret police in order to protect himself by reporting that a foreigner had asked "too many questions." A government employee who

looked like a harassed Ernest Borgnine rushed about giving
out the New Year's Eve program and explaining that they
were not following the exact order. (At our previous meeting, he whispered—as if there were a danger of being over-
heard—about a "desperate situation" facing the Copts, apolo-
gized for his rusty English and promptly added in a breathless
rush: "The Moslems have put everything into Arabic. I
never get a chance to use my once-beautiful English.") In
back of him as he distributed programs were crude paintings on the wall of the Coptic school showing British para-
troopers being machine-gunned as they landed during the
Suez attack. Shooting them down were young men and
women. Copts, of course.

Speaking for the president of al-Tewfik Coptic Benevolent Association, who was ill at home, a prominent Copt
told the audience: "We are celebrating this feast now in the
shade of the liberty and independence which we owe to our
great leader, Gamal Abdel Nasser, who made his policy of
neutrality and peace in order to maintain the independence
and integrity of the nation." Later, the archbishop noted
that the "martyrs of the Coptic Church had irrigated with
their holy blood the soil of the country" and he pledged
Coptic loyalty to the regime.

The audience listened with politeness but without enthusiasm, for it was a balmy summer night in Cairo with a
high reading in rhetorical humidity. The dignitaries—more
second than first-string in rank—were seated in front and
behind them, the distracted clusters of family units gave the
impression that they were only slightly interested in the duty
they were performing. These descendants of Pharaohs, these
sons of martyrs sat on folding chairs next to plump wives,
nubile daughters, and restless children, watching, as if in a
mirror, their own reflection on the stage.

They were watching the public Copt, reasonable, cautious
and cooperative, ready to acknowledge the justice, the wis-

dom and the strength of the ruling power. They echo Moslem indignation against the British and the Israelis, and if Nasser dresses Mohammed as a socialist, the Copts put similar clothes on Christ. Late in 1961 as the Nasser regime ballyhooed its "socialistic" phase and keyed it to the Koran, a leading Coptic priest lectured in Cairo's Journalists' Syndicate on the relation of socialism to Christianity. The head of the Coptic Seminary announced: "There is no Christian who doesn't believe in the socialistic life. True Christianity demands socialism."

The public Copt has an obvious resemblance to his unfavorable stereotype, but privately he is torn by self-doubt and confusion. He is uncertain about his ability as a Copt to face the current threat, and he is even confused about the definition of the threat. Publicly, he is the priest, the journalist and the government employee who have a face for New Year's eve celebrations and turn a worried private face toward the contemporary Coptic situation.

The private moods differ in their view of the severity of the Coptic crisis and the degree of rejection in at least four identifiable ways:

The attitude that all is lost; the Copts are heading toward oblivion.

The feeling that there are difficulties, but life goes on, and, anyway, there is a tendency to exaggerate our troubles.

The limited optimism based on a revival underway in the church.

The limited pessimism that "we are doing all right, but what about our children?"

The militants, closest psychologically to the martyrs' tradition, are the most pessimistic. A Coptic priest at the celebration of 1677 A.M. had said privately: "All is lost. Many people come to me with their troubles and the thing worrying them most is lack of jobs." A leading Coptic lawyer said: "We no longer believe in the possibility of coexistence between Copt and Moslem in Egypt. There will be no Copts left in three or four generations if things go as they are. For the Copts, there is nowhere to turn. If they turn outside, the Moslems will strike at them. If they turn to the Moslems they will be rejected."

These extreme pessimists blame Coptic timidity, ineffectual church leadership in secular affairs and disunity within the community. Other Christian leaders add that at times of crisis they have trouble mobilizing the Copts in a united Christian front against Moslem inroads on their prerogatives. At one meeting of Christian groups in Alexandria, a Coptic priest—criticizing his people but not failing to exaggerate their numbers—confessed in disgust: "I work every day for my people and they are not behind me. We do not have five million people; we have five million mosquitoes." Above all, the pessimists look upon the Copts as a community and the church as its instrument. Speaking of the Patriarch, who is obsessed with praying, both public and private, one Coptic priest complained: "It is not enough to pray all day; he must *do* things." The pessimists are convinced that religion alone cannot save the community, and that Coptic survival depends on the community.

However, many of the Copts who are established in the professions and in business have little contact with organized Coptic life. They are indifferent to a battle for rights where the lines are not clearly drawn and where their personal involvement seems remote. They are Copts with skills, who have competed successfully and carved out a personal niche in Egypt. They tend to see their less successful fellows as hypersensitive, ready to see discrimination behind every rebuff and they repeat malicious stories about the young Copt who applied for a job as a radio broadcaster and was turned down. "Why?" his friends asked. "Because I am a C-C-C-Copt," he stuttered in reply. These indifferent Copts point out that some of their best friends are Moslems, which only means that both communities have a meeting place in the twilight zone of the lukewarm Moslem and Copt. From the viewpoint of the Coptic community, these are the Copts who sap the strength of their group and also the ones with a great deal to sacrifice by becoming militant. They would be in danger of losing their identity, except that the Moslems are far from permitting this to happen. They will become militant when it is too late.

The hopeful Copts are inspired by religion and think of themselves primarily as members of the Church of Egypt. Their inspiration and optimism comes from faith in God, for as a Coptic priest, who was organizing a new church in Alexandria, explained: "If we have faith, God will open shut doors." A layman who was counting the priest's collection money after Mass in a converted gymnasium was asked how only 25 Egyptian pounds could enable the priest to accumulate enough money for a new church building. He replied without hesitation. "We never worry about completing a church. We just start building it. God will complete it."

Appropriately, the leaders of optimism and revival are not only close to the monastic tradition, they often are monks, heirs of the tradition of fleeing to the desert to pray and to be nourished by their faith. Lacking the combativeness of the extreme pessimists, they have spiritual resources and are able to see sunlight on an overcast day. Persecution becomes an asset. A priest explains: "As persecution increases, we will be more in power, in heart." A monk who is one of the most influential men in the Coptic Church called the pressure "helpful" because "it brings people who stayed away in touch with the church. They feel they are counted as Christians and must act as Christians."

Basically, their hopefulness stems from renewed confidence in the church and the encouraging sight of its revival. Born out of the traditional marriage of church and community is their hope that if the church thrives so will the community. Meanwhile, they face worldly problems by employing the traditional Coptic technique of fighting their wars without firing a shot. If rejected, they infiltrate; if frustrated, they try seduction. A priest, referring to the job problems of young Copts, explained: "If a factory has no jobs for Copts, it will still need engineers and will one day hire a Coptic engineer who will find a way to get jobs for other Copts." A church spokesman said that the antidote for the "negative feeling" of the young is jobs. "Our main aim is to get rid of despair. If Copts can't work in the government or national-ized companies, the thing to do is to create jobs by invest-ments in companies and businesses." In a town in Lower Egypt, a high-spirited Coptic priest described how well he gets along with local Moslem officials. "To keep away trouble, I send them little gifts on their various holidays. It only costs 20 pounds a year." Then he added the slogan of accommoda-tion that characterizes the hopeful and the pious: "You shouldn't take on battles you can't win."

The attitude of the partial pessimists—worried more about tomorrow than today—was thoughtfully articulated one eve-ning on the roof of a villa overlooking the Nile in a remote part of Upper Egypt. We drank Egyptian beer and used a pen knife to extract imported paté from its tin container as we watched the sudden disappearance of the sun that de-prives Egypt of lingering sunsets. Then came the night breeze after the heat of the summer day. Overhead a full moon. Below, the inky Nile. Absence of sound, presence of Egypt. In such isolated moments, when there is a sensation of being completely cut off from the rest of the civilized world, the non-Egyptian senses the strange, compulsive attraction of Egypt for the Egyptian. A Coptic architect explained his feelings.

"For the first time, my brothers-in-law, cousins, and friends are talking about where to go if it becomes necessary to leave

Egypt. What started us talking about it was all the nationalization which makes more and more people work for the
government where it is impossible to earn a good salary. And
the more the government controls, the less chance there is for
Christians." In the morning, the architect said: "Sometimes
I'm optimistic about the future. I don't know whether I
should think of going. I'm established, but my children are
another thing."

Copts who are worried about the next generation sense
the accelerated triumph of the Moslem orientation in Egyptian life. The present regime is not suddenly fanatical and
anti-Christian, but it does envelop much more of Egyptian
life than any of its predecessors. A Moslem-dominated, Mos-
lem-oriented government not only means that all things
being equal, the Moslems will have preference. It also means
that stress on achievement and skills will be lessened and
that the race in which the best man wins will be either discarded or it will be rigged. Moreover, Egypt's leap forward
in education has trained many more Moslems who can fill,
more or less, professional and technical jobs in which Copts
often were uniquely supplying a need. As Coptic skills and
training become less effective weapons of survival, more and
more Copts see discouraging signs that "No Copts need
apply."

By 1960, the march of government nationalization had
trampled on many industries and businesses where Copts
were in control or held the bulk of the professional and
skilled positions. Using the Congo troubles as a pretext, Nasser took over the Belgian holdings as he had acted against
British and French holdings after the 1956 Suez invasion.
He nationalized the press, the National Bank of Egypt, Bank
Misr, and the importing business in medicine, medical supplies, pharmaceuticals, and tea. For Copts all this was more
than nationalization, they felt as though they were reading a
series of eviction notices.

In July 1961, nationalization embraced all banks, insurance companies, utilities and other enterprises regarded as essential, a total of 259 companies. The cotton export industry had been nationalized the previous month. Other businesses, including the flourishing textile concerns, were ordered to yield 50 percent interest to the government. Ninety-one companies were singled out for appointment of government managers. Also, by limiting private ownership of stock, the government made it impossible for any individual to exert control over a private firm. According to Egyptian economists, the regime had now carried government control to 90 percent of the organized sector of the economy. Retail outlets, artisans and other small-scale enterprises were all that remained.

As long as the labels Copt and Moslem have personal consequences, government actions can never be regarded as neutral, and Copts complain that the present regime is widening irreparably the gap between the groups. Whatever takes place in Egypt, one universal minority question recurs: "Is it good for Copts?" For an outsider, personally involved in a different world, it is easy to become impatient with this community introversion, but more often there is a universal ring, an everyman's story in the stubborn persistence of the Copts and their determination not to lose their identity. Undoubtedly, the self-interest and narcissim have been strongly at work in maintaining them as an identifiable group in a usually unfriendly river valley of poverty and persecution. In one of the moments when personal impatience prevailed, I turned from a long, hot day of listening to the Copts to an indefatigable Jesuit who has spent a lifetime working among them. He offered me Turkish coffee and I asked him, "What are these Copts, after all?"

He shrugged his shoulders as he repeated the question. "What are the Copts? They are not only a church, not only a community, not only a race." Then he discarded conventional labels.

"They are a presence. They are here!"

Part Two:
Cross and Crescent

CHAPTER V

A Name in the Shape of a Cross

In the early part of the tenth century, the Caliph al-Hakim, who had a Christian mother and who claimed he was divine, carried on one of the most severe persecutions ever directed against the Copts. According to the Moslem historian Makrizi, "he then obliged every man among the Christians to wear, hanging from his neck, a wooden cross of the weight of five rotl (about five pounds), and forbade them to ride on horses, but made them ride on mules and asses. . . . He also ordered that the turbans of the Christians should be black . . ."

10h

≈ 5 lbs

Black turbans

Now, in the mid-twentieth century, the Copts of Egypt carry simpler Christian labels: often a cross tattooed on the inside of their right wrist and, almost always, their names.

When Egyptian newspapers printed the list of 400 members of Egypt's pre-arranged National Assembly in 1960, the Copts immediately counted names. Their tally was 13 Christians; they knew their own by their Christian first or last names. In about nine out of ten cases, the label is as reliable as the five-pound cross of al-Hakim.

The obvious consequence is that a Moslem or a Christian is readily identified in the most casual social situation, or in

43

any newspaper story. My good friends Ali, Omar and Mohammed could only be Moslems, for the former two carry the names of Moslem caliphs and the latter the prophet's name. For variety, there are 99 different names referring to Mohammed, other names of caliphs, honorary Islamic names like as-Sayyid (master) and names beginning with Abd al- (slave of) or similar variations. The Copts select the names of the Apostles, saints, angels, and any other Biblical figures; they also have a fondness for ancient Egyptian names like Isis. No self-respecting Copt would mislabel his newborn by giving him a distinctively Moslem name, and no Coptic priest would confer such a name at baptism. For the present generation of adult Copts, born when Christians dominated white collar and professional occupations, it was an advantage to have a Christian name as a calling card and only in recent years has a trend toward neutral names become pronounced. But even when a given name is neutral, the main Coptic family names are well known, especially when a family member achieves any renown.

Thus at the sight of 13 stray Christians among the parliamentary 400, the Copts turned their private face of despair on the turn of events and the gist of their complaint was: "There is room for only 13 of us even in that fake parliament which is nothing but a rubber stamp for Nasser."

Since the Copts know their own, it was also possible to get an authoritative rundown on their presence in high-echelon official positions. Excluding the rubber-stamp National Assembly, there were an estimated 150 top positions under governmental control in 1960. The total includes cabinet ministers, under-secretaries in the ministries, counselors of state, governors, rectors, vice rectors and deans of the state universities and colleges, members of the courts of appeal, and heads of nationalized banks. Among the 150, there were only three Copts: one cabinet minister, one university dean and a president of a Court of Appeals.

On this count, the Copts submit a compelling indictment. If the Coptic and Moslem communities had equal proportions of education, background and skill and only the laws of chance and bureaucratic selection operated, then the Copts, being about one out of six in Egypt, would inevitably do better than one in fifty. Moreover, the Copts, with their long tradition of skills and a high proportion of professionals and university graduates, would undoubtedly do considerably better than one in six. For the leading members of the Coptic community, the selection of those 150 is especially bitter, since many of the appointees leapfrogged over Copts who had outranked them.

A head count can be carried one step further into the other echelons of government, including those Egyptians chosen to represent the nation abroad. The Foreign Ministry is a crucial place to examine the Coptic-Moslem proportion, because personnel must be chosen for the ability to represent the country effectively as well as for trustworthiness. Consequently, the choice of the most suitable men reflects an official value judgment.

Though the acknowledged skills of the Copts in foreign languages and in dealing with foreigners would be expected to give them an advantage, a regular policy of excluding Copts undoubtedly prevails over all other considerations. The Foreign Ministry had 226 Moslems in Cairo, 5 Christians and 4 whose religion could not be determined. Three of the 5 Christians date back to the days of King Farouk. Of those assigned to embassies, legations and consulates abroad, there were 378 Moslems, 5 Christians and 4 unknown.

This head count was achieved without rifling the files of the Foreign Ministry but by bringing together the obvious: the Christian or Moslem label that every Egyptian carries in his name and the 1959 Egyptian Directory, a ponderous, detailed annual volume of 1,728 pages. The Directory contains a complete listing of the personnel in all government ministries and departments and any intelligent Egyptian can underline the Christian name and put a question mark over the neutral name that conceals the religion of its owner.

The 1952 Directory, the last one completed before the Nasser revolution overthrew King Farouk, offers cold comfort to the Copts, though it does indicate that exceptions to Moslem domination were more common. In a much smaller Foreign Ministry, there were 77 Moslems and 10 Christians, with 6 unknown. Abroad, there were 231 Moslems in embassies, legations and consulates, 7 Christians, 2 unknown.

The Ministry of Municipal and Rural Affairs, a large ministry at the opposite pole from foreign relations, has a much more favorable proportion, reflecting the success of Copts in areas where they can still market their skills and reliability. For instance, in this ministry, which has a large quota of engineers and inspectors, Copts comprise 20 percent of the personnel in its Department of Mechanical and Electrical Power. Including the Cairo municipality with the national ministry, there were 798 Moslems, 123 Christians and 12 unknown in 1959. The 1952 figures were 303 Moslems, 55 Christians and 1 unknown. This means that as the ministry tripled in size the ratio of Christians declined from one out of 6.5 to one out of 7.5.

Individual reports of abuses—more dramatic and less reliable—become common knowledge via the grapevine on which any group living under a dictatorship depends. Even with their layer of exaggeration, the reports are significant because they are believed by the Copts and feed their private mood. Sometimes the reports can be confirmed by Moslem sources, while the government's own sensitivity on the subject indicates there is much to conceal. For instance, it is reported that the 1959 government appointments for medical school graduates went almost entirely to Moslems. When examinations were held for positions with the National Center for Social and Criminological Research, most of those who passed were Copts; all of those who were appointed were Moslems. Promotions in the nationalized banks and their branches have overturned the normal considerations of seniority, experience and performance because of the large numbers of Copts in the ranks. A Cairo educator returned from Minia and Sohag, two of the main cities in Upper Egypt, to report that the Copts at the nationalized Barclay's Bank in both places were upset by the appointment of new directors. Whereas the staffs and the directors had always been Copts, Moslems now had been brought in at the top. A distraught young Copt told a mutual friend of the result of a special training course he attended in order to qualify for promotion in the government insurance company. After the course, the Moslems in the class were promoted; he was demoted. In one government-controlled company, a large number of Christians were fired, and one of them rehired. He had turned Moslem.

The situation can also be documented within the context of one large predominantly Moslem town off the Delta Road, connecting Alexandria and Cairo. There, a leader of the Coptic community stressed urgent bread-and-butter problems. The town has 14 cotton ginning factories, each with 200 workers and "at most there are 14 Copts in all 14 factories." He explained: "All the foremen are Moslems and they gather workers, all of them Moslems. You can be sure of that." If a Copt opens a shop in the town, he soon goes out of business because Moslems won't buy from him. When land was redistributed by the Nasser regime, only two Copts received land in the town's area and local officials have threatened them with the loss of their homes. Before you leave the town, you are reminded: "You can't feel the pressure, but we do. Because we live here."

The regime's handling of Liberation Province is revealing because the experiment was designed as a national showplace for everyone from junketing Western journalists to sympa-

thetic Afro-Asians. Before 1956, not one Coptic family was
settled in the utopian province, then four Coptic families
were brought in. They are still there out of a total of 400
families. Other Copts have been brought in for their professional, technical or white collar skills: two doctors, a sani-
tary inspector, the hospital director, 12 engineers and 300
employees, a total of about 350 Copts in the specially-se-
lected population of 12,000 at Liberation Province.

Throughout the country, land reform has benefited Moslems almost exclusively, since local officials are all Moslems and have been left free to guarantee the selection of
Moslems. When a prominent Egyptian from the heavily-
Coptic city of Assyut was asked how he knew very few Copts
were picked to receive land that was taken largely from the
area's Coptic landowners, he replied with the assurance of
any Middle Easterner who knows his community and of the
Copt who knows his own: "How do we know this? We know
the people who received the land."

The mechanics of preference are similar in Egyptian companies whose directors (or personnel managers) are Moslems; otherwise, pressures come from government inspectors
and official supervisory agencies. Mentioned too often to be
ignored is the unwritten "official order" that the proper
proportion of employees is ten Moslems, one Christian in
order to approximate the official population proportions.
The consequences can be an upheaval in the country's economy since the Christians have long predominated in business,
technology and in administrative activities generally.

A Christian owner of a company reported a revealing dialogue with a government inspector after the latter had
checked the list of laborers, who were all Moslems, and administrative and technical employees, who were all Christians. Referring to the latter, the inspector said:

"How many foreigners do you have working for you?"

"None. They are all Egyptian citizens."

"Are you sure they are all Egyptians? I would like to see some Mohammeds and Mahmouds on your list."

This story and many others like it abound in the Coptic community as reminders that the Moslems are on the march economically as well as politically. In the give-and-take of majority-minority competition, the communities follow their orientations. When Copts refuse to hire Moslems, they argue that they can find no Moslems who are both reliable and competent (which is not the whole truth). When Moslems put pressure on company managers, they demand that special efforts be made to hire Moslems (which is not entirely fair). For the Copts, accustomed to defending their position, the size of the threat is reflected in the alarming number of Copts who have surrendered. They have killed themselves as Copts and have converted to Islam. While many convert to get an easy Moslem divorce, a large number do so in order to get jobs. A fairly reliable estimate is that 5,000 Copts become Moslems each year. Reflecting the job and divorce motives, the converts are generally men between 20 and 40 years of age, which means the community's loss must be multiplied by the children of these lost Copts.

As the pattern of exclusion becomes more pronounced, Coptic unrest is intensified by a comparison between today and yesterday. They are not only disturbed about the latest fruits of the grapevine of complaint, but they also suffer from the relative deprivation of a minority whose position has been drastically undermined in the lifetime of its adult members. The trend affects all levels as fewer and fewer Copts are being hired at the bottom and the top is confined to Moslems, so that both young Copts and those in mid-career see the door of opportunity either shut completely or only slightly ajar. The sound outside that door is the cry of the Copts.

CHAPTER VI
Signs of Equality

On the iron fence in front of the main railway station in Alexandria there is a sign faded by the sun; inscribed on it is the official Egyptian arithmetic of Moslem-Coptic relations. A painted Coptic cross and a painted crescent are joined by a plus sign. An equal sign shows the sum total in Arabic as "wahda" (unity).

The arithmetic lesson has been applied most energetically by the present Egyptian government during times of crisis when the public Copt is mobilized and the country's ranks are ceremoniously closed. The regime has never had trouble arranging national unity demonstrations in the tradition established by nationalist leaders after World War I; the Copts cooperate. But tactically-minded Copts warn that cooperation is sold without promissory notes. Concessions or guarantees from the government are not obtained and opportunities for improving the minority position are lost. Whereas Coptic leaders, embracing caution, feel that such cooperation has avoided trouble or at least postponed it, the Moslem regime is confirmed in its attitude that Copts as a group can be manipulated. The Moslem masses, conditioned to public charades, endure another performance.

When the international crisis touched off by Egypt's nationalization of the Suez Canal was approaching a climax, word was passed to the Coptic Church that an inter-faith "unity" rally should be held October 3, 1956, two days before the U.N. Security Council debate on Egypt's action. The rally, called the Coptic Community Conference, was held at the headquarters of the Coptic Patriarchate and was attended by various Christian leaders and such Moslem dignitaries as the Minister of Waqfs (religious endowments) and the Mufti of Egypt. Iskandar Dimyan, the lay head of the Coptic Community Council, called upon the Security Council to hear the views of the Egyptian people, since "certain Western politicians" had been attempting to sow dissension among Egyptians. He emphasized that the "entire Egyptian nation" stood behind Nasser. One of the five resolutions passed at the conference announced:

To inform the U.N. Security Council immediately that the Coptic Conference held in Cairo today, representing Egyptian Christians of all denominations, strongly deplores the flagrant transgressions against Egyptian sovereignty and confirms their support of Gamal Abdel Nasser's policy to defend Egypt and her rights against any aggression. The conference is certain that the Security Council will, in the interest of world peace, sanction Egypt's act of nationalizing the Suez Canal Company.

There was little else in the newspaper accounts cleared by the government censor. However, an Egyptian involved in the arrangements described how the Coptic hierarchy worked energetically to do the government's bidding. An aide of the Patriarch personally brought into line a reluctant Christian leader, who had no intention "of licking Moslem boots," by promising that the Copts would not do so. His reluctance changed to cooperation, ended in disappointment.

Of those who spoke, only one addressed himself to the issue which overshadowed Suez in the private worries of the minorities, though his words were not reported in the Cairo press. A participant recalled that an Egyptian Catholic priest who is famous for his work among both Moslems and Christians rose to face the audience crowded into the court-yard of the Patriarchate. The red-and-white turbans of Moslem sheikhs were visible everywhere, looking from the platform like warning signals for anyone who would stray from the night's script. Behind the priest were Moslem dignitaries and the Christian and Coptic leaders whose words, by contrast, made him sound like some poor player who had forgotten his lines.

"Now that the foreigners are gone, we are like a family," the priest said. "I watched Egyptian pilots taking ships through the Suez Canal and I was proud. Now that our foreign guests are gone, we can look at our internal problems. If we look into the minds of Christians, we see that there is a feeling of disquiet and so we must work for peace of mind. Christians must remain Christians, Moslems must remain Moslems, and they must all be linked in order to keep the landscape beautiful as a landscape containing a variety of flowers."

In underlining the anxiety within the Christian communities, he had violated the rule of public silence both accepted by the Copts and imposed upon them by the Nasser regime. The Copts did not want to hear such words on their platform. In challenging the Moslems to do something about the anxiety, the priest was asking them to admit the existence of a problem they won't acknowledge. They did not want to listen.

The late Grand Rabbi of Egypt, Dr. Haim Nahum, was away at the time, but upon his return he went immediately to the office of the Presidency to thank Nasser for letting him go abroad for medical treatment. He also thanked the Ministers of Finance and the Interior for letting him take enough money out of Egypt to pay his doctor bills. The Grand Rabbi denied the existence of religious persecution and said of the Suez nationalization: "We support and bless this step."

After Israel, France and England attacked Egypt in the fall of 1956, the arithmetic of religious brotherhood was summed up in various officially-sponsored gestures of unity. Even as gestures they symbolized the existence of some bargaining power on the part of Copts and other non-Moslems; otherwise the government would not have bothered with the gestures. In fact, since that peak year of crisis, the gestures have fallen off drastically, underlining the obvious: the optimum bargaining time for the Copts is a national crisis when the regime needs the open support of all Egyptians. When Egypt is embroiled in international politics, the appearance of happy minorities is also important for a propaganda position abroad, but the Copts, wooing the reluctant Moslem majority, have not taken advantage of their bargaining position at such times.

On November 27,1956, the Ministry of Interior acted to counter, in particular, the reports of expulsions of Jews and confiscation of their property. A spokesman denied that any order had been issued "to expel any Egyptian from Egypt or dismiss him from his job or to interfere in his activities in any way, no matter what his religion." The press highlighted feature stories and pictures of Jews thriving in Egypt and a "loyalty" telegram from a Jewish lawyer was widely publicized. Then it was the Copts' turn. Coptic priests preached sermons in three Alexandria mosques and arrangements were announced for an exchange of visits between imams of mosques and Coptic priests. The sermon at a leading Cairo Protestant church was given by the Minister of Waqfs, Sheikh Ahmed Hassan al-Bakury. In mid-December, a joint delegation of Egypt's leading Coptic and Moslem religious leaders visited Nasser and put the following message on record: "We greet the President of the Republic and emphasize the unity of the country against the aggressor-usurper and despotic imperialism. We also renew our pledge to work hand in hand in the service of the dear Fatherland." That same morn-

ing, the acting Coptic Patriarch and a number of bishops also
visited the rector of al-Azhar University, the center of orthodox Islam, to return his visit a few days earlier to the Patriarchate.

These gestures, demonstrating manipulation of all religious leaders, Moslem included, could point the way to a
constructive campaign for unity. Government prodding of
religious leaders, if continuous and determined, would improve relations between majority and minority. The learned
Moslem theologians, the sheikhs and ulema, must take their
cue from the regime in all their sermons and they can be
prodded to take as their sermon text the sign at the Alexandria railway station. And important government leaders,
even the president, can reenforce the impact of such a campaign with gestures and examples that set the style. However,
the official policy of religious brotherhood reduces itself to a
demand for universal political support for the regime. If the
majority religion is put at the disposal of the state, then a
minority religion can not expect to remain aloof. Egyptian
Copts, living in Moslem Egypt, have learned this lesson and
bid for acceptance every time they try to be more royal than
the king.

In August 1960, the Coptic Church once again walked in
the shadow of the learned men of Islam who met at al-Azhar
University to support a Nasser propaganda tempest over
Iran's commercial dealings with Israel. Nasser called such
dealings tantamount to recognition of Israel and the learned
theologians of Islam held a conference and passed resolutions denouncing the Shah of Moslem Iran for violating the
teachings of the Koran, Allah's word revealed to Mohammed.
The Coptic Patriarch then ordered Sunday sermons in all
Coptic churches to denounce the Shah's recognition of Israel
and he told his flock, who ordinarily think of Moslems in
connection with religious fanaticism: "The existence of
Israel can be considered a constant threat to world peace,

which is one of the basic tenets of Christianity. This is because Israel is established on religious fanaticism which di-
vides the world into religious camps which are now conflict-
ing, instead of being founded on closely related humanitarian
groupings. States that are modern leave religion to God and
make the homeland depend on the citizens and their politicians." Then the Patriarch directed his representative at
the meeting of the World Council of Churches to make a
proposal. But it was not about the situation facing the Copts
in 1960; it asked the Council to denounce a nation established in 1948.

In the required exchange of curtsies between Moslem and
Copt, even Hassan al-Bakury, a former leader in the mili-
tantly anti-Christian Moslem Brotherhood, took his place in
line while he was Minister of Waqfs. The occasion in the
spring of 1956 was the publication—by his ministry—of a
book entitled *The Rights of Man according to Islamic Law*.
The Coptic bishop of Assyut promptly protested that the
book was an attack on Christianity published by a government ministry; the Minister of Waqfs responded by with-
drawing the book from circulation and by promising that
government censors would thereafter carefully screen all
books issued by his ministry. As publicized in the government-controlled press, the letters rang with brotherhood.

Wrote the Moslem minister:

I know we are in great need of unity and must stop any preju-
dice in this world full of attacks on religion. Anything that might
provoke a rift between Christians and Moslems will harm both
Islam and Christianity. Any action that might develop the spirit
of forgiveness and pave the way for adherence to religion will
benefit both Christianity and Islam.

Replied the Coptic bishop:

We received with admiration your letter which showed most
profound sentiments and the spirit of humanity and forgiveness.
We did not doubt when we sent our letter to you that we were

addressing a benevolent heart and a good government taking
care of its people and protecting religion against those who
abominate it and who are full of misleading ideas and subversive
attitudes. The book we complained about pained us, but your
letter assured us that real nationality is above every other con-
sideration and that the nation, which is made up of both Christians and Moslems, is more important than anything else.

In one legal clause or another, this policy of prejudice-free
nationality has been formally endorsed in the various constitutions of Egypt. It was clearly set down in the post-independ-
ence Constitution of 1923 and in the post-revolutionary Constitution of 1956. After the 1958 merger of Syria and Egypt
into the United Arab Republic, Article 7, Part III, of the
Provisional Constitution echoed other constitutions: "All
citizens are equal before the law. They are equal in their
rights and obligations, without distinction of race, origin,
language, religion or creed." It is just as the faded sign in
Alexandria indicates.

CHAPTER VII

A Question, Mr. President

President Gamal Abdel Nasser laughed good-naturedly at the question posed during his appearance before a group of touring Syrian and Lebanese emigrants. Asked one of the visitors, practically all of whom were Christians: "Is there any discrimination against Christians in the UAR? One of the papers in America said there is, but I don't believe it."

As he laughed, President Nasser said, "Neither do I believe it. I have here beside me at the conference table a Christian minister. He might be the one to answer your question."

Then Dr. Kamal Ramzy Stino, UAR Minister of Supply and a Copt, told the visitors from America that he knew their country well, having studied for five years at California universities. He was reassuring: "I would like to tell you there is no discrimination of any kind against Christians or any favoritism for Moslems in the United Arab Republic. Christians here occupy top positions and they are doing big business. There is no restriction of any kind against their activities or freedom."

The visitors applauded the answer and Nasser added in the spirit of Cross and Crescent: "I consider myself responsible for all the people in the UAR without distinction.

When we were fighting Jews in Palestine, the Jewish bullets
didn't discriminate between Moslem and Christian soldiers.
I think if we look at everybody in terms of his religion, this
will only lead to civil war. I don't look to Christians or Moslems here as Christians or Moslems, but I consider them all
citizens of the UAR."

Like a hypochondriac mulling over the painful symptoms
of a malady with real and psychological causes, the troubled
Coptic minority fixed on this casual question-and-answer incident of the summer of 1959. To many Copts, Nasser's
cavalier handling of the question, his avoidance of a denial
of discrimination, and his use of the public Copt as a puppet
were symptomatic of his refusal to treat their problems with
sympathy or serious attention. It was also a public confrontation which no Copt would dare to make; the following summer there were no questions and no answers for the touring
emigrants.

In fact, the first American correspondent expelled from
Egypt, Barrett McGurn of the New York "Herald Tribune,"
had been reporting on the plight of non-Moslems in Egypt
in the aftermath of the 1956 attack on Suez. The Egyptian
government accused McGurn, who is regarded as one of the
most competent U.S. foreign correspondents, of writing
"complete fabrications." McGurn later wrote:

For two months I rooted through the facts of economic decay,
discrimination against Jews and Christians, and hardships for
foreigners of almost every stripe, and slowly laid bare a picture
of weakness and confusion that conflicted painfully with the vain-
glorious portrait which the national radio was giving to Nasser's
hungry people and to the awakening Arab nationalists of the
Middle East.

Also in the background was McGurn's contact with "Rayon
d'Egypte," a Catholic weekly whose Jesuit editor complained
in print about the treatment of Christians. The Jesuit was
expelled to his native Lebanon and the paper suppressed.

The Copts, who have no home but Egypt, view any Egyptian government from the perspective of their position. They watch, analyze and discuss Nasser's strongly-centralized rule, using shreds of evidence, imaginative invention, straws in the wind, and the harvest of the grapevine. Because Nasser is the ultimate power in Egypt, the Copts try to probe his mind and his mentality, and in the end they usually indict him for sins of omission, rather than commission, for what he permits, seldom for what he does. And the touchstone as always: "Is he good or bad for Copts?"

One Sunday afternoon in a large town in Lower Egypt, a Coptic priest described what Copts expected of the President of the entire Egyptian nation. He began by discussing those around Nasser:

"They want the country for the Moslems. I personally feel the revolution is a good thing, but there are many people just beneath Nasser who have come into power and who have the same attitudes as the Moslem Brotherhood. Now that the country is well-organized, it's not like before. When these men under Nasser give an order, it gets done . . . I'll tell you what Nasser can do. He can visit Coptic churches; he can visit the Patriarch. He can send gifts to the Patriarch and he can take him along on official occasions. When the little people see what their chief does, then they will be different."

From all that can be surmised, Nasser is indifferent to the Coptic situation. One Catholic missionary, while discussing Nasser and the Christians, was swishing a horse-tail fly whisk back and forth when its long, black hairs caught his eye. He blurted out: "You might say the Christians are like flies to Nasser. They are little annoyances that he chases away." Of the many published studies of Nasser, none reconstructs his biography in the perspective of the Coptic minority. As summarized one evening alongside a private desert swimming pool by a Westernized Egyptian whose days of comfort probably will not be inherited by his children, the biography mixes the facts with psychology, rumor, instinct and intuition.

"Begin," he said, "in the village of Beni Mor, about two miles northeast of Assyut, in the area of Upper Egypt where the Copts are stronger than anywhere else. One-third of Beni Mor's population of 5,000 is Coptic; its great landowners were Copts. This is the home town of Nasser's family, though Nasser was born in Alexandria and spent his entire childhood and adolescence in Lower Egypt.

"In Beni Mor, the Coptic religion is not very appetizing. Its clergy is in a low state, more concerned with money than prayer, and each year when the pilgrims come to the village's church to honor St. George, there are bloody sacrifices of animals and quarrels about money. Even if Nasser did not experience all this, you get an idea of how his attitude toward the Copts was influenced by his family.

"It is said that when Nasser was a child, he once jumped on the running board of a car in which a rich Copt was riding. The Copt told his chauffeur to dispatch him like 'an Egyptian fly.' Whether or not the story is true, you can see the resentment that was caused by the rich Coptic landowners among the Moslem lower classes. And don't forget Nasser's family was 'Saidi'—from Upper Egypt—provincial poor, and the young Nasser could not grow up without drinking in resentments.

"Do you know who threw the big dinner for Nasser when he visited Beni Mor after coming to power? It was the big landowner in Beni Mor, a Copt. (The Assyut-Beni Mor estates also were among the first hit by land reform.)

"Nowhere in his childhood experiences did Nasser meet Copts of strong qualities and his biographers never mention any books about religion in his reading. He knows nothing about Christianity and when as President he visited the outside world—Moscow, Yugoslavia, Indonesia, Greece—he never saw the church held in high esteem. Nasser's behavior toward the church is not as someone hating it, but he looks on it as an anachronism. He regards the Coptic Church as a secondary problem."

Nor does Nasser have much patience with defiant clergy, as he demonstrated to Egyptian Catholics. In 1959 when the Catholic Patriarchs of Lebanon, Syria and Egypt sent a letter of protest to Nasser on the treatment of Christians, he ignored the letter, except to send his representative to a diplomatic reception at the Vatican embassy with a message that he was "angry." Fifteen months later, when the Lebanese ambassador paid a courtesy call on Nasser before returning home for a vacation, Nasser snapped: "Tell your Patriarch I'm angry. I thought he was my friend." The ambassador's Maronite Patriarch, His Beatitude Paul Meouchi, was regarded as conciliatory during Lebanon's 1958 civil war; some Christian fanatics even called him pro-Nasser. Taken aback, the Lebanese ambassador suggested a meeting between Nasser and the Greek Catholic Patriarch of Egypt about the fifteen-month-old letter. Nasser promised to do so upon the ambassador's return, but the meeting never took place.

In late 1955 when Egyptian Catholics were planning a protest, Nasser sent a verbal message to certain bishops, according to Associated Press correspondent Wilton Wynn. "Let me assure you that we will not tolerate religious fanaticism, no matter from what quarter," the message said. "The Moslem Brotherhood tried it, and you know what we did to them. Remember, you are not nearly so strong as were the Moslem Brothers."

Nasser's combination of impatience and indifference toward Christians has nothing to do with piety as a Moslem. U.S. mass magazines and newspapers have featured pictures of Nasser in white robes prostrating himself during a pilgrimage to Mecca; one magazine saw piety in the fact that he fingered Moslem prayer beads during an interview. His

pilgrimage to Mecca was political expediency after his rise
to power and a bid for popularity; the prayer beads, sometimes called "nervous beads," are used by Christians as well
as Moslems with about the same religious feeling and function as chewing gum. Nasser, in his personal buildup into a
charismatic figure, has drawn on all possible psychological
resources to lift up a backward, hungry nation and to make
it follow his orders. Since Moslem Egyptians have such strong
feelings for Islam, he has used Islamic fuel to motivate them.

During Nasser's greatest time of crisis in November 1956,
while Cairo underwent British bombing, he drove to the
mosque of al-Azhar, symbolic center of Islamic learning, to
rally his countrymen. The mosque was crowded with thousands of worshippers, inside and outside, who had gathered
for Friday prayers on the Moslem holy day. The faithful sat
cross-legged for four hours on the intricate Oriental carpets
of blues, reds and gold as they heard Nasser invoke a simple
message of national glory from the platform where they ordinarily receive their weekly message from the Koran. A week
later, Nasser returned to al-Azhar to report that the crisis
was over, that "the whole world is now with us, even free
people in Britain herself. Egypt is united, strong, and mono-
lithic, determined and resolved." By implication, at least,
both episodes at al-Azhar had ignored the four million Egyptians who are not Moslems.

Within Nasser's inner circle which encloses all real power
in Egypt, there are none but the fellow Moslem army
officers to whom he gravitated in forming his secret group of
plotting army officers. With self-re-enforcing loyalty, the ruling clique has never expanded. The nominal Coptic representative in the UAR cabinet, Kamal Ramzy Stino, has only
an administrative position and is the medium through which
Nasser makes his wishes known to the Coptic community.
To a certain extent, Stino, a former university professor,

presents Coptic complaints, but he is a bystander in the regime.

Granted Nasser's indifference to the minority problem in Egypt, it is not surprising that government officials have a loose rein in regard to religious intolerance. Nasser reportedly has assured the Coptic Patriarch that he would personally correct any situation where injustice is called to his attention, but a court of last appeal is too remote from a constantly changing situation. In the absence of cues from Nasser, the Moslem militants in his regime enjoy a permissive atmosphere as long as they do not upset the regime's policies and plans. The Copts see their community being pushed gradually downhill toward oblivion, but since they are not tottering at the edge of a cliff, community leaders hesitate to cry loudly for help.

Groping through this web of Coptic-Moslem relations can be a frustrating, sometimes exasperating, ordeal for the outsider, who possibly is the only one who can retain the necessary perspective. The trouble is that the current Coptic-Moslem situation lacks the clear-cut, gory ingredients of melodrama. There are so many international examples of harsh, bloody repression of minorities that the postwar world tends to be indifferent to the slow death which threatens a minority unable to parade its wounded onstage. Yet in that slow death there is something antiseptic and coldly up-to-date, for the Copts are a minority being ignored to death.

The Coptic experience with the Ministry of Education illustrates their position vis à vis the Moslem-dominated regime. The ministry is headed by probably the most militant Moslem in the Nasser inner circle, Kamal Eddine Hussein, who is described as a soldier with a field officer's rank and a sergeant-major's mentality. As Minister of Education, Hussein, who once worked closely with the Moslem Brotherhood, is blamed for tying Cairo University into political knots and for creating an atmosphere of Moslem militancy in the ministry supervising Egypt's expanding educational system. While the Copts are at a loss to document a complete indictment, it was possible to get a picture of how discrimination operates in the ministry's handling of grants for university study abroad, the dream of Egyptian students. The Copts working on this program, as in other parts of the government, are limited to the operational level and excluded from policy and decision making. They are close enough, nevertheless, to see a pattern that is growing throughout the Egyptian bureaucracy.

A Moslem sociologist, in describing his own disillusionment with the system of awarding foreign study grants, recalled a conversation with a former head of the Education Ministry section which makes the awards. The official admitted that all things being equal, Moslems were automatically chosen and that openings for grants had been canceled when it was found only Christians applied. On one occasion, a recipient of an anthropology fellowship came to the social scientist asking for advice in planning his university studies. He began: "First, tell me what anthropology is."

In one government list of approved grants for foreign study, only 25 of the 227 recipients were Copts, and according to those working with the program, the list had been rigged in favor of Moslems. It is easy to see how the system can be channeled to flow in favor of Moslems and against Copts. At each of several stages between application and selection for study abroad, the applicant faces interviews by government committees. The stated criteria are the needs of the country, the available funds from UAR sources or outside aid and the value to the government, since each fellowship holder must agree to work for the government for about twice the number of years he studies abroad. At each stage, selection involves intangible value judgments by Moslem-dominated screening committees.

Some known miscarriages in the process show what is

happening. One Coptic doctor, with "very good" grades and all other qualifications, was rejected as first choice and made a second alternate behind two Moslems with "good" grades. When the Copt started a law suit to protest the decision, he discovered that the grant money was used up before any action could be taken. He was told "to come back next year." In engineering, a Moslem applicant with "fair" grades was made a fifth alternate and two Copts third and fourth alternates. In this case, the Copts prospered because the fifth alternate was the son of a government minister so the winner of the grant and five alternates were awarded scholarships. (Ordinarily, alternates receive grants only when those ahead of them default.) Another Coptic engineer, who applied for two different grants, received one, but flunked his oral interview for language fluency on the other. Processing was immediately stopped on the grant he had received. Then the candidate, protesting vigorously, presented an irresistible argument: the committee testing his English had practically the same members in both interviews. How could they pass him the first time and flunk him the second? (His school work in English had been rated B-plus, well above the usual grade of applications, which was C-minus). In the end, he was permitted to study abroad, but the anti-Coptic moral seemed clear. There is no way of drawing up a list of particulars, but the growing pattern of such incidents has a multiplier effect. It is distributed via the Coptic grapevine, creating the self-conscious burden of discrimination that Copts carry on their shoulders. It is part of the invisible suffering.

In the spring of 1959, Minister of Education Hussein showed his hand when he turned a rambling, inchoate book by an obscure Coptic schoolteacher into a cause célèbre. The name of the schoolteacher, Nazmi Luka, still sounded like Benedict Arnold on the lips of Copts many months later. His children had been beaten en route to school, his home required a police guard and his name was smeared with the label of traitor whose pieces of silver were a schoolteacher's promotion. The charge: writing a book praising Mohammed at the expense of Christianity. Not only did Hussein write the introduction to the book, but he ordered it used in the schools of Syria and Egypt. That included Christian schools, which was the equivalent of ordering a book banned by the Pope to be studied in U.S. Catholic schools or a book of Catholic apologetics to be read in a Lutheran school.

In the book *Mohammed, the Prophet and the Message*, Luka traces the contribution of religion to mankind before the arrival of Mohammed and in the characteristic style of a popular Arabic tract he moves from one sweeping generality to the next. He discusses the Old Testament and ancient Israel under the theme "Religion of a Nation" and Christianity under the heading "Religion of the Heart." Then, he reports, the "people needed a new religion" (Islam) that "must go to all people without discrimination regarding nations, descendants or classes."

In the final chapter, Luka lays down a challenge to his fellow Copts, an ironic challenge since he did not act on its implications. Luka remains technically a Copt, though he concluded: "Whatever religion is preached after Islam, it will not reach its peak of glory. There is no doubt about it. Any man who doubts the truth of this prophet [Mohammed] is lying to himself. Peace unto him [Mohammed] for what he has done for mankind. Before he came, people were following the wrong path, but he put them on the right path. Peace unto those who say the truth."

On the cover of the school edition were these inflammatory words: "The Ministry of Education has decided on the study of this book in its schools in the Northern [Syria] and Southern [Egypt] Regions." Hussein said in his introduction that "the idea for this book had come to the heart of an Arabic Christian" who had written it as "a brick in the foundation of a single thinking and spiritual unity which would join our people in a common faith with God, the One; a faith with common virtues, common human ideals and with spiritual values." Sixty-five thousand copies of the book were printed for school distribution and public sale, an unprecedented printing in the Arab world where authors celebrate if they sell a thousand copies.

In Syria, Christians held a book burning and in Egypt even the Copts joined Catholics and Protestants in an organized protest. The compromise that was arranged provided for retention of Luka's book on the official textbook list, but excluded it from the required matter for school examinations. In effect, this meant Christian private schools could ignore the book, though the schoolteacher's exercise in Moslem appreciation lighted a fire of indignation that still burns. As far as the Copts are concerned, Moslem militancy again showed its hand at the highest level of government, recalling the constitution proclaimed for the Republic of Egypt on January 16, 1956. Part I, Article 3, was explicit: "Islam is the religion of the state and Arabic its official language."

The juxtaposition of Islam, the Arabic language and the state is no zealot's whim, but another manifestation of the predominance of Islam. To Moslems, Arabic is the "language of the angels" as well as their prophet and there is a strong feeling that non-Moslems can not master it properly. Christians are even discouraged from entering the Arabic literature department at Cairo University. One influential Westerner, who recalled his successful efforts to obtain admission for a Christian into the department, said he had to make a personal phone call to the Minister of Education. "Egyptians say real knowledge of Arabic comes only through knowledge of the Koran," he said. "One minister of education even confided that there is an unwritten law in his ministry that the Arabic language is for Moslems, not Christians."

The Copts, in turn, have gravitated toward the Western languages, especially the French taught by the good nuns and Jesuits at their excellent schools. It is not surprising to find a Coptic housewife whose Arabic is limited to the kitchen talk needed for servants and whose education with the nuns included two class periods a week of Arabic and the remainder in French, including recreation periods.

With the Arabization of all schools under the Nasser regime, Arabic, understandably, has replaced French in private schools. Since the Koran is regarded as the paramount vehicle for the Arabic language, all students get massive exposure to the sacred book of Islam and the official curriculum assigns different sections of the Koran by class levels. The Copts denounce this as proselytizing, since the class time devoted to mastering the complexities of the Arab language, the Koran included, is indeed large. A 1956 UNESCO report found that Arabic language study took one out of every three class hours during the first four years of school, one out of every four hours in the fifth and sixth years. The government does, however, make religious instruction mandatory in all its schools, so that Christians study their religion in two one-hour lessons weekly in primary school and one hour weekly in secondary school, with the exception of the final year. In practice, this usually means Coptic teachers on the school staffs are ordered to teach religion in addition to their regular duties, though in most cases they are ill-prepared.

But it is in church building that government resistance particularly irritates the Copts, for their religious affiliation is often so symbolic that the church dome may mean more than prayer. It is like raising a Coptic flag on the horizon. No Coptic churches have been closed by the government, nor is permission to build churches refused. The required building permits face delay after delay, applications are entangled in red tape and regulations are applied to the smallest obstructive detail.

In the Upper Egyptian city of Minia, there is a hole in the ground which symbolizes Moslem militancy and the frustrated plans of the city's 30,000 Copts who wanted to build a cathedral. Money was collected, 16,000 pounds (about $45,000) paid for the land, and excavation work begun. But the head of the government school located nearby complained to Cairo that it was improper to have a church so near her school. As a result, permission was never granted for the cathedral. Passing by in one of the horse-drawn carriages that serve as the city's taxis, the visitor to Minia moves slowly down a quiet street in the midday heat of summer and sees not a person stirring, not even the guard at the Coptic hole in the ground, which is surrounded by a brick wall.

When U.S. socialist Norman Thomas toured the Middle East in the fall of 1957, he asked Nasser point blank whether there was discrimination against Copts. In vehemently denying the existence of discrimination, Nasser cited high government and diplomatic posts held by the Copts. He added that three-quarters of the engineering students at Cairo's new Ain Shams University were Copts.

Nasser saw the specter of "Coptic fanaticism" which he feared would cause a counter-reaction of "Moslem fanaticism" and he said that the Coptic community had tried on numerous occasions to interfere with legislation drafted by his regime. In Nasser's view, the Copts had to overcome their obsession with discrimination if they were going to adjust to the New Egypt.

Nasser might even have added that the Provisional UAR Constitution of March 5, 1958, discarded the designation of Islam as the state religion. This reportedly was done out of deference to the militant Christians of Syria and to conform with the international style of legal brotherhood.

When Mohammed Naguib, the fatherly general chosen as the figurehead of the 1952 Egyptian revolution, was interviewed by a New York reporter whom he knew to be Jewish,

he opened his desk drawer and pulled out a Torah. He told
the reporter that it was a gift from the Jewish community
and added: "I regard all Egyptians, whatever their color or
creed, to be equal. On my wall at home I have, hanging
beside several quotations from the Koran, a Christian religious picture given to me by a Coptic priest." Naguib, whose
Christmas card depicted a Christian church, a mosque and a
synagogue side by side against a Cairo background, used to
turn up at services in the various Christian churches. One
Yom Kippur he attended services at the Ismailiya synagogue
and one Christmas Eve in the Evangelical Church. Naguib
wrote in his autobiography: "Both as prime minister and as
president, therefore, I have had to go to great lengths to
persuade the minorities that the new Egypt will be as toler-
ant as any state in the world."

In the early days of the revolution, posters were put up
stressing national unity. One poster had a picture of a church
near a mosque and bore the caption "Religion is for God
—and the country is for all." More than eight years later, in
February 1960, Nasser laid the first stone for a Carmelite
convent and declared: "Religion is for God; the nation is
for all citizens." In late August 1961, Nasser said: "We in
our republic don't even acknowledge the existence of discrimination. We look at everyone in our society as a citizen
having rights and duties. In proportion to his capacity, we
give each citizen a chance to work and we do not distribute
jobs on the basis of discrimination." When Nasser made the
first statement, Egyptian Christians commented that it was
the only declaration of religious equality they could recall
in any of his speeches, and it was made in Syria. The second
statement was addressed to a visiting delegation of Syrian
youths, and after September 28, 1961, the Copts noted that
Nasser's Syrian audience of militant Christians was no longer
in the United Arab Republic.

CHAPTER VIII

The Brotherhood of Moslems

On Sunday morning, February 20, 1910, at the height of the Cairo social season, "the first genuine Egyptian who had risen to the highest position in the country" was entering his carriage when a fanatical pharmacist shot him to death. The victim was Butros Pasha Ghali, the prime minister who had been called the first genuine Egyptian in the post by the British overlord for Egypt in his annual report the year before. He was referring, of course, to the fact that the pasha was a Copt.

Two days before the assassination, Prime Minister Ghali, who never concealed his sympathy for the British occupation, had introduced a bill to extend the Suez Canal concession. While Ghali was a Copt, the hand that held the gun throbbed with the mixture of nationalism, xenophobia, and Moslem fervor that still characterizes the Arab fanatic. After the assassin, who was named Wardani, was sentenced to death, the sentence was questioned by the Grand Mufti and the Moslem religious court because the murder weapon, a revolver, is not mentioned in Moslem law and the next of kin had not joined in the prosecution. Added to these atavistic legalisms was the one-sided argument that "a Moslem slaying a pagan does not render himself liable to the death penalty."

Copts and Moslems in Egypt came into this century with such mutual distrust that the vernacular press was filled with the kind of vituperation that leaves no doubt the Mufti's arguments were read with a straight face. One sample from contemporary Moslem reactions to Coptic activities was set off because a political party had been formed under the aegis of a few Copts. Swelling up with characteristic Arabic vituperation, the commentator wrote in the vernacular press:

That faithless gang organized by some low-class Copts which has fallen upon its country like an unruly son which attacks his kind mother . . . The punishment of such a gang should be that they should be kicked to death . . . They still have faces and bodies similar to those of demons and monkeys, which is a proof that they hide poisonous spirits within their evil souls. The fact that they exist in the world confirms Darwin's theory that human beings are generated from monkeys. You sons of adulterous women, you descendants of the bearers of trays, have you become so foolhardy that you should start and abuse the Moslem faith? The curse of Allah on you! . . . You tails of camels with your monkey faces, you bones of bodies, you poor, dreaming fools, you sons of mean rogues! Is it with such acts that such people win renown?

Such was the inflammatory tone of much of the Egyptian press that Moslem tears were for the assassin who was executed, while the Copts mourned their short-lived prime minister. As it turned out, Wardani was a prominent member of the Mutual Brotherhood, a band of terrorists who early in this century foreshadowed another brotherhood that still casts a shadow over the Coptic minority in Egypt. The latter-day group, the Moslem Brotherhood, repeated history even to the extent of another assassination plot.

The similarity of both brotherhoods extended to a plan to infiltrate the army, that persistent trump card in Egypt. A letter taken from an associate of Wardani spoke of entering "the army with a view to sowing the seeds of patriotism among the officers and men. Effort must be made to get as many educated youths, such as physicians and officers of the Military School, admitted to the army, so that this small army might side with us and not against us." Early in 1954, when Nasser outlawed the Moslem Brotherhood, he complained that its "crime was to have tried to introduce itself into the police and the army, with the object of gaining control of them in order to seize power by force. They were trying to start a kind of holy war against us."

On October 26, 1954, a Moslem Brother fired eight badly-aimed shots from a .36-caliber Italian revolver at Nasser as he addressed a mammoth crowd in Alexandria's Liberation Square. The 1910 killing of the Coptic prime minister was a symbolic act of Moslem fanaticism; the death of Nasser would have radically rearranged recent Egyptian history. As a result of the unsuccessful assassination plot, the Moslem Brotherhood was crushed, a boon for the Copts who regarded the Moslem fundamentalists as the personification of anti-Christian feeling. The Brotherhood had poisoned the air with such examples of its mentality as a special song with these lines: "One religion and not two religions/No Cross after now." The Copts were hearing a slogan which meant that it would be the Christians' turn after the Jews: "Today is Saturday/Tomorrow is Sunday." Nasser also used the opportunity to implicate Mohammed Naguib in the plot and to remove him as the regime's figurehead, which diluted the blessing since Naguib was more inclined than Nasser to promote Coptic-Moslem harmony.

The success of the Moslem Brotherhood, which was founded in April 1929, in Ismailiya, had been marked, sudden and frightening—as far as the Copts were concerned—after the group's transfer to Cairo in 1933. The Brotherhood's aim was not merely a state religion, but a religious state built on the Islamic religion, whose principles would dominate all aspects of life. The Moslem Brothers were not merely militant Moslems; they were fanatics. They even threatened to bomb the headquarters of the Arabic edition of the *Reader's Digest* unless its editor became a Moslem and propagated Islam. The acknowledged mass appeal of the Moslem Brotherhood was reflected in membership claims of two million; during Nasser's trial of Moslem Brothers, a half million and 200,000 were other membership figures mentioned. Monthly dues amounted to 10 piasters, a good day's pay for Egyptian peasants.

Though the motive for Nasser's suppression of the Brotherhood was its threat to his regime, he did thereby perform his single, forceful act of reassurance for the Coptic minority. Basically a reaction to the sense of inferiority and inadequacy which Moslems felt in the face of modernism and the West, the Brotherhood was leading Moslems in an armed and violent retreat to a remote social, economic, legal and political fortress in order to defend the Koran. Its list of evils included imperialism, political parties, usury, foreign companies (and by extension, Christian companies), the dress of women, infidel foreign movies, depravity and degeneracy (by implication, modernism). But the Brotherhood aim was not annihilation of non-Moslems; it was subjugation. Christians and foreigners had a place in Egypt, a subordinate one, and on this point in particular the Brotherhood appealed to the Moslem masses.

The Supreme Guide of the Brotherhood once told Associated Press correspondent Wilton Wynn: "In a purely Moslem state, minorities are our guests. And a good Moslem will fight to the death to protect his guest." Officially, even the Moslem Brothers upheld the theoretical unity of Cross and Crescent, even to public speeches espousing the brotherhood of all Egyptians. They, too, shared the regime's view of official equality, though from the statements of both Copts and Moslems, as well as the autobiography of Mohammed Naguib, the testimony contradicts them; undoubtedly, the Moslem Brotherhood was out to crush the Christians economically, politically, socially. Their Egypt would be no partnership, and non-Moslems would have to accept a country by, of and for Moslems.

The taste of persecution, which the Moslem Brotherhood left behind, still is on Coptic palates. Copts see the spirit, if not the body, of the Brotherhood marching on and point out that the Nasser revolution cooperated with the Brotherhood from the beginning. In the plotting stage, Nasser's aides worked closely with Brotherhood leaders, who were offered portfolios in the post-revolutionary cabinet. When political parties were suppressed in January 1953, the Brotherhood was untouched on the grounds that it was not a political party; its influence on the leaders of the revolution and on the army was apparent. When a Constitutional Committee of 50 leading Egyptians was formed, it contained 6 Copts and as many known Moslem Brothers. Until the attack on Nasser, many Copts expected the Moslem Brothers to dominate the regime. There was talk of an official program to evict Copts from government and business, from education and finance.

Some eight years after the shots were fired at Nasser, leading Copts describe the situation as basically unchanged, though it lacks the formal leadership of the Moslem Brothers. Copts say this because of the Moslem-Christian animosity that has fluctuated in intensity between the Mutual Brotherhood assassination of 1910 and the Moslem Brotherhood attempted assassination of 1954. The Copts are convinced that the Moslems can never accept the non-Moslem as a full and equal partner in the nation. With few exceptions, when Moslems speak of Arabs, Arab unity, Arab nationalism, Arab revival and the other labels in their litany, they are thinking of fellow Moslems. It is mainly the

Christians of the Middle East who extend the coverage of the label Arab to include themselves. For Moslems, the term applies only to those who believe that the mission of Mohammed is the central fact of history.

For the most part, the Moslem attitude stems from their belief in the superiority of Islam. The "people of the Book" (the Bible) are tolerated because both Christian and Jewish revelations are regarded as valid—up to a point. In the Moslem view, they are imperfect and incomplete revelations, superseded by the message of Allah's last and greatest prophet, Mohammed, who left Moslems with the final and perfect form of Divine Revelation. Thus, under no circumstances, could Moslems regard other religions as equal nor could they help but place other religious communities in a secondary position.

While the situation is blurred in large urban centers with fashionable Coptic sections, the stratification is obvious in the villages, where non-Moslems are at the bottom of the social ladder no matter how wealthy they are. A recently-published government study of the village of Beni Smei, about 20 miles southwest of Assyut in Upper Egypt, separated the 8,000 villagers into four levels that were described as typical:

First level: Moslem families descended from Ali al-Fil, a descendant of Mohammed, who came to the village centuries ago. These families occupy the highest social level, regardless of their wealth.

Second level: Moslem families not descended from Ali al-Fil, achieving status from their size, wealth, early arrival in the village or intermarriage with the first level.

Third level: The rest of the Moslem families. They are usually small families in alliance with a first-level family.

Fourth level: Coptic families, no matter how wealthy, are placed in the lowest status by the village's dominant Moslem majority. Thus, an impoverished, illiterate Moslem fellah descended from Ali al-Fil can be at the top of the social ladder and a Coptic merchant, with a bank account in Switzerland, a book account in Paris and a university degree, at the other end.

Beni Smei, chosen for the government study because it typifies the blood-vengeance code still operating in Upper Egypt, also provided little-known information on how Copts receive personal protection from Moslems against other Moslems. Under the system, which recalls the Moslem Brotherhood remark about fighting to the death for a guest, each Coptic family attaches itself to a Moslem family known as "the Arab protector of the Christian family" and the Moslem family assumes the duty of avenging the murder of any member of the Coptic family. The avenging Moslem family not only murders in retaliation, but also becomes liable to the counter-retaliation in the chain reaction of revenge that goes on for decades in Upper Egyptian villages. The Copts assist their protector by providing guns and money, but never take a direct part in the revenge. In case of conflicts between Moslem families, the Copts act as carriers of news, as well as suppliers of guns and money, but they always remain on the outside.

The Copts thereby purchase protection without loss of life and without danger to their strong economic position in the village. Traditionally non-violent, better educated, and lacking a vengeance code of their own, the Copts are in too vulnerable a position to participate. It also requires little imagination for Copts to realize that murder is bad for business. On the Moslem side, the system of inequality is re-enforced, for if a Copt had the acknowledged right to retaliate personally against a Moslem, he would be accorded a position of equality. The eye-for-an-eye code is designed for exchange of blood between equals and so the Moslems are not willing to acknowledge a Copt's right to kill a Moslem. Though Copts are close-mouthed about their affiliation with a Moslem family as a precaution against provoking ill will, the protector of every Coptic family is well-known in the village.

However, government researchers found that if a Coptic family suffered a murder at the hands of its protector-family, no revenge is demanded. In one such case, the father of the Coptic victim visited his son's murderer to congratulate him on his release from prison—such is the precarious position of Coptic villagers. When Copt kills Copt, revenge is not usually sought, and on the rare occasions when Copts seek revenge against each other, professional Moslem murderers are hired. The government report added: "No case was found of a Christian killing a Moslem, so the situation in such a case is not known. But more than that, the villagers were unable to imagine that a Christian could kill a Moslem."

The distance between the atmosphere of Beni Smei and the upper echelons of traditional Islam is no further than the carrying power of the statement by the Grand Mufti of Egypt when he was asked a few years ago about Christians who became Moslems. He said: "A Christian who embraces Islam is not an apostate; he is merely recognizing the Prophet in addition to his Christian faith. He is adding to and perfecting his faith. Whereas a Moslem who becomes a Christian is denying Mohammed; he is an apostate and deserves to be put to death."

Psychologically, the heart of Islam in Egypt is al-Azhar University, to whose mosque Nasser went in time of crisis and whose hand-picked rector energetically hunts up Koranic verses to support Nasser policies. As far as one of Egypt's most prominent Copts is concerned, "As long as al-Azhar is here, there always will be fanaticism." Certainly, al-Azhar has been the citadel of rigid, unchanging Islam, more concerned with preserving archaic forms than in developing a modern approach. It has opposed women's suffrage and any modification of the crippling Ramadan fast, blocking modernization with literal and reactionary interpretations of the Koran. Shut up in their medieval hideaway, al-Azhar's faculty and thousands of students intensify the shadow of Moslem intolerance under which non-Moslems live.

Nationalism in Egypt, as elsewhere in the Middle East, has had a choice of tying itself to Islam for emotional, psychological and ideological support or of promoting a secular patriotism which separates nationalism from religion. In theory and in its constitution, the Nasser regime has chosen the latter, but in practice the ruling clique, composed of Moslems from the lower and middle classes, has viewed the nation in an Islamic framework. Rather than oppose any tide of Moslem militancy, the regime has worked to channel it, sometimes to swim with it. The eager courtship and reluctant suppression of the Moslem Brotherhood, the psychological alliance with al-Azhar and the public obeisance to Islam have intensified the Moslem tone of the government, though political strategy may be the main motivation. Nasser's calculated reading of the Egyptian masses is that overwhelmingly they share the mood of Beni Smei and the Grand Mufti. Though intellectuals and liberated Moslems are critical of Islam's traditionalism, few ever raise their voices in public against it.

Cutting the cloth of Islam to suit his regime, Nasser can take liberties with Koranic interpretation and use religious leaders to second his motions. He has decided, in effect, that the ruler of Egypt must have the Koran working for him and that the elusive and often contradictory document left behind by Mohammed can be tailored to any style. On July 23, 1961, when Nasser announced his wholesale nationalization of the economy, he made it clear that Lenin was not the inspiration for his action. He declared that Mohammed was the first to call for a policy of nationalization, that Mohammed was the father of the "first socialist state." Nasser has said in a personal interview that the regime is "anxious not to do anything contrary to the Koran." In harping on the word "Arab" he gives every indication he means "Moslem." " 'Arab' is a disguised word for 'Moslem,' " a Coptic lawyer argued. "Nasser uses 'Arab' because 'Moslem' is too blunt and too inflammatory."

In re-enforcing the brotherhood of Moslems, Nasser excludes the "true Egyptians" who stand outside the mosque and complain. The Copts point out that this is not the way to develop a modern nation, especially when a skilled and extremely useful large minority are turned into outsiders. They add that Islam should be encouraged away from anachronism and toward modernism by removal of religious intolerance. They warn that the Nasser regime has mounted the dinosaur of Islam and they don't see how the regime can ride it to success in modernizing Egypt.

CHAPTER IX
Personal Matters

Among the many leaders that speak for a troubled minority, a few take an Olympian view of the entire landscape, which includes both majority and minority. At a June 16, 1953, meeting of the committee drafting a constitution for Egypt's new regime, the voice belonged to a courageous lawyer, Farid Antoun, and he tried to make himself heard above the sound of the Moslem Brotherhood. Antoun, who was the Copt chosen to serve in Naguib's cabinet, addressed himself to an Egypt where patriotism and religion were separate:

"It is true that we must take note of the sentiments of the majority, but I believe that our mission is to establish a Constitution whose object is a resolute society. We ought, therefore, to have an approach that is realistic, logical and practical, without bringing in religion. . . . I would like to specify that we are not summoned to make one religion prevail over another, but to pursue the interests of all Egyptians in the light of practical and logical considerations without religious interference. . . . In regard to religious devotions, each is free to pursue them, whether in his home, in his mosque or in his church."

The response came from a voice of orthodox Islam, Abdel

81

Qadir Awda, a leading Moslem Brother who had set down the intellectual charter for the movement:

"My honorable colleague wishes to establish a constitutional principle devoid of religion."

Antoun: "I have not said that it was necessary to rid oneself of religion."

Awda: "I wish to say that the honorable member sanctions a cutting loose from religion."

Antoun: "I ask my honorable colleague to give me the opportunity to set down specifically the view I am putting forth. I say that the goal of the Constitution is to proclaim the common interests of all Egyptians. These interests are obtainable by the light of reality, from the need and common goal of all citizens . . . We can therefore acknowledge established principles without reference to religious justification, but instead rely on logic, experience and the public interest."

In retrospect, this encounter takes on the quality of melodrama. On one hand, the lawyer for the plaintiff Copts, and on the other, counsel for the dominant Moslem majority that was both defendant and judge. There is also a double postscript to the encounter. In 1960, Farid Antoun defied a civil court by standing up to a Moslem court official who called him a "kafir" (infidel). On December 8, 1954, Abdel Qadir Awda died on the gallows as one of the six Moslem Brothers liquidated by the regime after the attempted assassination of Nasser.

Employing a lawyer's tactics in 1953, Antoun argued for complete freedom for his client—freedom from the Islamic straitjacket for Copts, and Moslems as well. Barring that, he would accept a limited guarantee in terms of protection for the personal status regulations governing Coptic marriage, annulment, divorce, custody of children and inheritance. The system stems from the millets which the Ottoman Empire set up as administrative units along religious lines to administer the civil affairs of each religious group. The rules of personal status were determined by the various religions for their membership, and the Egyptian legal system still honors these rules of the religions. An Egyptian is bound legally by his group's rules from birth to death, whether or not he believes as his father did, unless he evades them by changing his religion.

Because religion and community were merged in Islam any attempts to separate church and state run afoul of fundamental Moslem tradition. Also basic to this tradition is the notion that, while each religion can run its own community affairs, the Moslem community is paramount, its regulations have priority, its members a special position. Buried in Antoun's harmless-sounding generalizations was a radical attack on the privileged position of the Moslem community and an indirect plea for protection of the non-Moslem communities. Awda, whose Brotherhood regarded the Koran as the most suitable constitution for Egypt, was determined to keep Allah as dominant as possible in any constitution drawn up by the committee. The conflict can be unraveled in steps:

1. Under the apparently innocent principle that the Moslem community is superior, its rules apply in cases where a Moslem is involved with a non-Moslem.

2. The door is wide open for any Egyptian to become a Moslem in order to take advantage of the rules for Moslems.

3. The heart of any community, especially a beleaguered minority, is the family, and widespread application of Moslem rules would devastate Christian family life. The Moslem right to have four wives is a doubtful privilege that practically all Moslems have the sense to avoid, but divorce is another matter. Islamic law provides for the easiest divorce in the world; the husband need only register before witnesses the fact that he has discarded his wife.

4. Antoun was arguing, in effect, for a revolutionary change in this open-door policy, for he would remove the

benefits of the conversions of convenience which take advantage of Moslem regulations. He would prevent a Copt from getting an easy Moslem divorce by changing religions.

In the case of a Copt who tires of his wife, it is a simple matter to become a Moslem, obtain a divorce merely by registering the dissolution of the marriage and even obtain custody of the children, since in such cases the court automatically favors the Moslem as a more suitable parent. Militant Moslems do not want to close the door on such conversions of convenience which are both an increasingly serious threat to the Coptic community and an opportunity for Moslem expansion. Antoun would close this door and require Copts to stick to the regulations under which they marry. At a subsequent constitutional meeting, Antoun made it clear how he favored going further—a single marriage and divorce law for all Egyptians to replace the religiously-constructed legal mosaic. "At the last meeting, my colleague Abdel Qadir Awda said that I wished to free myself of religion, but I reassured him as I reassured Anba Yuannis (a Coptic prelate). I say to them that I am not referring to religious precepts that are Islamic or Christian, but I am examining the question of the family from a specifically social point of view." Antoun's plea would not be startling in the Western world, but he was standing face to face with the rigid, inflexible expression of Islam in Egypt. He favored laws to strengthen the family by limiting all Egyptians to one wife and by severely restricting divorce.

In one recent case where both Coptic husband and wife invoked the conversion technique, the bizarre possibilities were illustrated. The wife became a Moslem in order to be free of her husband, since Islamic law does not recognize the marriage of a Moslem woman to a Christian. The husband retaliated by turning Moslem and gaining custody of the children under the Islamic preference for the father. Next, the wife applied to court for permission to visit her children.

But meanwhile she had reverted to her Coptic religion. Permission was denied.

A Moslem girl who fell in love with the boy next door and married him described the consequences and the confusion because he happened to be a Copt. Her father, an engineer, is a "little conservative"; he observes the Ramadan fast but doesn't go to the mosque. When he heard of their secret six-year courtship, he became angry for two reasons: his daughter was dating unchaperoned and the date was a Copt. He forbade her to go out, except when accompanied by her mother, brothers or sisters. Meanwhile, at the young man's house, his father threatened to disinherit him if he married the Moslem girl next door.

After the young man's father died, the couple set a date for marriage. When the young man went to the girl's home, her father said he would give permission only if he converted to Islam but the young man refused, and the couple ran off to marry in civil court. In the nine years since the marriage, the girl has never seen her father or brothers, though she meets her sisters and mother outside her family home. Nor has she visited her husband's family home.

Two years after the civil marriage, the girl became a Copt, entered her name on the church registry and was married in the Coptic Church. The Coptic priest advised her not to register the change of religion with the government lest she suffer reprisals. She explained: "It is against Islamic society for a Moslem girl to marry a Copt. But it is all right for a Moslem man to marry a Coptic girl, since our Nabi [Prophet Mohammed] took a Coptic wife."

When her husband went abroad for advanced professional study, the couple ran into more problems. The wife's identity papers say Moslem and single; her conversion was only to satisfy the church's ban on a priest marrying a Copt to a Moslem. Her passport is based on her identity cards, and with the tight restrictions on exit visas, she can qualify for travel only as the wife of a student. Her passport says otherwise, so she is spending three years alone while her husband completes his special studies. As this plump, good-natured Moslem-Coptic woman described the ups and downs of her romance and marriage, she was matter-of-fact, occasionally jovial. As I sat there listening on a hot Cairo afternoon it all sounded so natural, not like Romeo and Juliet, but like an unavoidable Egyptian boy-girl story when the couple is separated by the legal-religious barrier.

There are other complications. Theoretically, any Moslem can get a court order forbidding a Moslem woman to live with a Copt. In practice, a Moslem woman married to a Copt can get a certificate from the church that she is a Copt and usually this will be enough to avoid legal troubles. The children of such a marriage are technically illegitimate, though this seems to be more a potential than a real problem. If the husband dies without a will, his wife can not inherit his property; in intestate cases, no inheritance is possible between Moslem and Copt, though this barrier can be hurdled if a will is written. A few years ago, the wife of a prominent Copt was unable to inherit her husband's wealth because he had turned Moslem as a business convenience three months before he committed suicide. Since his wife remained a Copt and he neglected to write a will, she was cut off without a piaster.

A Coptic lawyer who works in this twilight zone of Coptic-Moslem legalisms offered the following opinion:

"From a religious point of view, a Moslem can not renounce Islam and become a Copt. For in becoming a Copt, he is regarded as dead. It is not clear in Egypt which prevails in a conflict, religious or constitutional principles. The latter says all Egyptians are equal and suffer no disadvantages due to religion; the former places Moslems in a favored position."

According to the Cairo Office of Registration of the Ministry of Justice, which records conversions, the number of registered conversions to Islam in the Cairo province is modest: 195 in 1956, 242 in 1957, 180 in 1958 and 191 in 1959. Since each administrative area keeps separate statistics that are not reported to a central office, an official nationwide figure is not available. Moreover, such data is normally released only to government employees having a letter certifying that it is needed for official research; clearly the government wants to avoid troublesome reactions to what is a sore point between the communities. Moreover, the Registration Office reports, contrary to popular belief, it is not against the law for a Moslem to become a Christian. (Though in doing so, a Moslem cannot use the change to juggle his personal status rights, if he finds that it is advantageous in a pending court case.)

The conversion procedure is officially prescribed. On appearing at the provincial office to report his intention to convert, a Copt fills out two forms, one of which is sent to the Coptic Patriarchate. There is a two-week waiting period in which the Coptic Church tries to convince its defecting son to remain. One official meeting between a priest and the convert takes place in a government office, though informal contacts are made in order to remove the two main reasons for conversions, a desire to get a job or to facilitate a divorce. Of those signifying their intention to become Moslems in the Cairo province, about one out of three Copts are persuaded to hold fast to their community. For those who persist, a Moslem sheikh hears their pronouncement of belief in Islam and signs the statement of belief as an official witness.

Once a Moslem, an Egyptian has the benefit of the personal status regulations of his new religious community, but there is almost never any indication that change of religion was accompanied by change of faith. The Copt has changed his community in what none deny is a calculating transaction, even a cynical one, except for the fact that some con-

verts are so lukewarm in their commitment to the Coptic
Church or community that they are exchanging one form of
indifference for another. For others, economic pressures or
emotional demands overcome their Coptic commitment.

Until 1956, personal status was so intimately bound up
with religion that the religious communities had their own
courts for handling such cases. Moslem courts handled those
cases in which the two parties were from different communities; even if both were Christians, the Moslem courts
would handle the case if one were, for instance, Greek Catholic and the other Coptic. Then Moslem law would apply,
except in the cases of divorce where the Catholic ban on
divorce was made applicable to both parties. Copts could
obtain divorces on the following grounds: adultery, three-
year separation, cruelty, or if a wife were barren or a husband impotent. Though it was not excessively difficult for
Copts to obtain such divorces, they still had to face the court,
establish grounds, carry on a legal battle for the children
and face lifetime alimony. A Copt who became a Moslem
got his divorce by registering it, had little responsibility to
his wife and was automatically awarded the children. Some
modifications were introduced in the fall of 1960, requiring
a Moslem to go through a court of law in registering a divorce and requiring fair provisions for the divorced wife.

Besides the confusion compounded by this maze of variations, another element was added to the system of religious
courts. It was corruption and scandal arising out of widespread reports of bribery of judges. On the face of it, abolition of the religious courts, announced September 21, 1955,
was a progressive move, turning over all cases to the civil
courts which would then apply the rules of all religious
communities in a uniform and regulated manner. However,
the government statement on the delicate matter of divorce
by conversion was disappointing to the Copts:

Changing religion means that persons will have the new rights authorized by the new religion. Changing religion in order to get a divorce or run away from marital obligations is something that happens all over the world. The man does so by choosing the religion by which he can benefit most. Some people emigrate from one country to another in order to run away from these obligations. For instance, Italians go to France for divorces. In the U.S., some people cross state borders in order to get the benefit of different divorce laws. The law can not do anything about people who follow devious ways.

While the Copts argue that the law certainly can provide for the devious ways of men, it is clear that the Moslem majority is not going to fight the Coptic battle to maintain its community and family life. The Copts are, in effect, seeking Moslem guarantees against wayward Copts, while the Moslems refuse to give up the traditional priority of the Moslem community, even for opportunistic converts. Moreover, when the new arrangement was put into effect early in 1956, the Copts discovered that the Moslem religious courts were directly incorporated—judges and clerks en masse—into the civil court system, while the Christian courts were abolished and their judges put on the shelf. Modernization had entered through the front door, while the tradition-bound Islamic court officials walked in through the back door, sat down and administered the rules for Christians as well as Moslems. And, as always, a man or woman could upset his community's regulations with a sudden conversion to Islam.

The situation went full cycle in the summer of 1959 for Farid Antoun, who had argued in 1953 for an overhaul of the Egyptian legal system. He went to court as his sister's lawyer when her husband became a Moslem in order to get an automatic divorce. In a heated court exchange over this divorce by conversion, the voice of traditional Islam was heard from a Moslem sheikh converted into a civil servant from his previous post in a religious court. The sheikh,

standing beside the newly-converted husband, called both
Antoun and his sister "kafirs" (infidels). When Antoun responded to the provocation in a much stronger manner, he
was held in contempt of court. For several months a threat
of prison hung over his head until he was finally censured
and allowed to go free.

Unlike Antoun's previous legal fencing with Moslem
Brother Awda, this encounter was private as far as the public
records are concerned. It never appeared in the newspapers,
though Antoun is one of the most important Copts in Egypt.
It was not even possible to see Antoun in order to discuss
the case. It became an "Egyptian secret"—well-known, often
discussed in private, but never publicly acknowledged.

Part Three:
The Pursuit of Survival

CHAPTER X

A Crisis in Leadership

While Nasser increased his power in Egypt, the Copts had the misfortune of having a weak Patriarch in the Chair of St. Mark. Demonstrating his celebrated sense of timing, Nasser moved in two directions on September 21, 1955. On one hand, he aroused the Copts by abolishing the religious courts, while on the other, he approved the banishment of their Patriarch, Anba Yusab II, which pleased the Copts and also underlined their lack of leadership. It was an inopportune time for the Copts to protest abolition of the religious courts, though they ultimately did so in a bold postscript to the Patriarch's banishment.

The Coptic crisis in leadership was personified by Anba Yusab, a pious churchman who could not rise to the demands of his role as Patriarch. Yet, according to the processes of any church bureaucracy, he was well-prepared by commitment and experience. Anba Yusab had joined the church at the age of fifteen as a monk in Upper Egypt and after a time was sent to Athens for four years to complete his studies. It was there that he learned Greek, which he spoke along with French, Arabic, and Coptic. In 1912, he became abbot in the Coptic monastery at Jaffa; in 1920 archbishop of

Guergueh in Upper Egypt. He was sent in 1930 as the Patriarch's personal representative to crown Haile Selassie as Ethiopia's Conquering Lion of Judah. From 1942 to 1944, Anba Yusab was acting Patriarch, and on May 27, 1946, he was enthroned as Patriarch, beginning a reign which coincided with a turbulent political period in Egypt.

The verbal, physical, and, finally, legal attacks made upon the Patriarch reflected the deep frustration felt by the Coptic community and the disappointment with their pope. Their traditional expectation that the Patriarch be a strong father-image was violated by the weak, indecisive figure of Yusab. It was as if the weakness of the father showed up the weakness of the family to the embarrassment of all the children —who, meanwhile, were fighting among themselves. The heated argument in the Coptic community followed these lines:

The body (the church) needed its head (the Patriarch). But if the head is abnormal, it will destroy the body.

Overwhelmingly, the Copts favored cutting off the head as the way to save the body.

The grey eminence in the situation was the Patriarch's valet, a fellah named Melik whom Yusab hired while he was Archbishop of Guergueh. As the Patriarch became more feeble, the valet became his go-between with bishops, priests and laymen. He became a chancellor of favors and appointments and it is generally believed that he engaged in a lucrative traffic with priests and bishops seeking advancement. Of the nineteen bishops appointed by Anba Yusab, it is rumored that as many as sixteen bought their appointments through the valet. Responsible Coptic sources also reported that a civil suit was pending in the city of Sohag between the valet and a Coptic bishop who allegedly never completed payment on the I.O.U. he signed in exchange for his appointment. The valet is said to be the owner of four buildings in Alexandria, three in Cairo, and to hold from various bishops

I.O.U.'s totaling 21,000 Egyptian pounds. As the unlettered, but shrewd, valet became the Patriarch's most influential advisor, he acquired influence over policy and administrative decisions affecting the entire Coptic community.

The reaction was strong among both laity and clergy, splitting the community over the issue of removing the Patriarch. Ethiopia, whose pious Coptic emperor was sympathetic toward the prelate who crowned him, complicated the situation by favoring Anba Yusab. Internally, the Copts bickered and feuded over the issue. Community leaders were at odds with bishops; clergy conspired with laity. Reports were widespread about corruption in the religious courts; price tags were placed on bishops' appointments as defamatory stories about the Patriarch embarrassed the Coptic minority.

At a low point in the crisis, a group of militants took matters into their own hands and kidnapped the Patriarch. The militants acted under the banner of the Umma Coptya —Society of the Coptic Nation—formed as a counterpart to the Moslem Brotherhood in zeal, though not in power. Organized by a young lawyer, Ibrahim Hilal, its aim was to revive the Coptic language, fight for political power and rejuvenate Coptic nationalism. It had its own uniforms, even designed a flag for the "Coptic Nation." The tone of its program was puritanical; the means included force. Just as the Moslem Brotherhood tried to remove Nasser from the scene after being outlawed, the Umma Coptya moved against the Patriarch after its official suppression March 23, 1954.

Two days after the July 23, 1954, anniversary of Farouk's overthrow, a group of Umma Coptya militants forced Anba Yusab II to resign at gunpoint with the anniversary threat, "Resign or your end will be like Farouk's." The night-time action, which was climaxed by a kidnapping, had a touch of Gilbert and Sullivan. The Umma Coptya had gone to the Patriarchate late at night, overcome the police guards, disarmed them and locked them up. They confronted the Patriarch in his room and ordered him to resign. When he refused, they threatened him until he gave in, using the official seals of the church to certify the resignation. Commandeering a taxi, four of them hustled the newly-resigned Patriarch off to a monastery in Old Cairo and then returned to the Pariarchate. (The taxi driver complained later that they refused to pay their fare for the round trip.)

After the kidnapping, the Umma Coptya assembled in the Church of St. Mark at the Patriarchate and roused the crowded Coptic section surrounding the Patriarchate by ringing the bells of St. Mark at 3:30 a.m. The conspirators intended to announce the Patriarch's resignation to a crowded church just before dawn and to present church, community and government with a fait accompli.

But the police intervened. The large crowd drawn to the Patriarchate was kept outside the walled enclosure, while the Umma Coptya commanded the Patriarch's headquarters and church within. The police hesitated shooting their way onto sacred territory, especially with a crowd of Copts surrounding them, so the government sent the Coptic Minister of Supply, Gindi Abdel Malik, to intercede with the Umma Coptya. He pleaded with them to avoid a shooting battle with the police and they finally gave in. Thirty-six militants were arrested on the spot; the rest scrambled over the wall and escaped. Eventually, 86 were arrested and charged with kidnapping and use of threats to kill as well as "apprehending four policemen and two detectives."

After the kidnapping, arrests, and return of Anba Yusab, the Umma Coptya, whose popularity had been limited mainly to young Copts, especially in Cairo's Fagallah section, ceased to function. Its founder is still under police surveillance. One of his followers, interviewed after his release from prison, was located through a series of intermediaries. After scrupulous examination of foreign passports and repeated assurances, he talked about the Umma Coptya's early days. He reported that early in the Nasser revolution, the regime approached the group, seeking cooperation, but the Umma Coptya refused to come to any understanding. Then spied upon and finally outlawed, it went underground to oppose the Moslem Brotherhood and to further the Coptic cause. "Nasser's principles are those of the Moslem Brotherhood," he said. "We wanted the Patriarch to create jobs for Copts, to open factories and businesses for unemployed Copts. But the Patriarch was weak. He had no personality, no strength of character." Squirming uneasily in his chair, the young man symbolized the bankruptcy of the Umma Coptya, rejected by the responsible elements in the Coptic community and shadowed by the secret police. It was a depressing encounter, the militant who started as a daring youth ended as a timid outcast. He held up a nicotine-stained finger. "I fear even my own finger."

The Umma Coptya program of violence was not only out of character for the Copts, it was doomed for practical reasons. In planning a test of strength with the Moslems, the Umma Coptya was clearly taking on an unequal fight which it was bound to lose, and in defeat it could invite a heavy penalty for the entire Coptic minority. Beginning with the Umma Coptya premise that the Moslems were in a holy war against non-Moslems, Christian violence would occasion even greater Moslem repressions. The dreams of its leader were also far-fetched; he once told a Coptic priest: "In six months, we will take over the government."

The Umma Coptya drew attention to a fundamental weakness in any Coptic campaign of militancy. The most powerful and most important elements in the community are also the most reluctant to fight. Wealthy and well-established, they have the most to lose by becoming activists and antagonizing the regime. For instance, the present Coptic Minister of Supply has many relatives highly placed in government

jobs; the head of the Coptic Community Council is a wealthy
contractor who can only prosper with government good will.
It is not surprising, then, that the most important Copts are
the most "reasonable" in dealing with the regime. The
Umma Coptya attracted the young men of the community,
those with the least to lose and also least able to mobilize
general support. Both desperate and powerless, they are the
segment of the community which is experiencing the greatest difficulty in getting jobs and is supplying many of the
converts to Islam.

Finally, when the Patriarch was officially banished, this
was accomplished because church and community leadership
joined forces. Previously, the Community Council had opposed any meeting of the Holy Synod of bishops unless the
Patriarch had acted as chairman. This made banishment
impossible without his consent. To support this position, the
Patriarch issued a statement citing Articles 2 and 7 of the
laws of the Holy Synod and obtained the endorsement of 15
bishops. The two laws interlocked, requiring the Patriarch as
chairman and requiring the chairman's approval for any action taken by the Holy Synod.

But another interpretation prevailed at the Synod meeting
which finally banished the Patriarch; the oldest bishop according to time of ordination was declared the legal chairman. The Synod's banishment decision was immediately
endorsed by the Community Council and on the next day,
September 21, 1955, the Coptic Minister of Supply Gindi
Abdel Malik announced: "The government has agreed to
relieve the Patriarich of his powers in response to the wishes
of the Coptic people and the leaders of the church after all
agreed that His Eminence is not fit to carry out his duties."

Within a week, the sickly and dispirited Patriarch was
sent to the Upper Egyptian monastery of al-Muharraq, revered as the site of the Holy Family's home in Egypt, and a
triumvirate of bishops elected to run the church until his

death. The three bishops were chosen at a joint meeting of eighteen members of the Community Council and twelve bishops and promptly approved by the government. Under this leadership, the Copts then confronted the other half of the regime's action of September 21, 1955—abolition of the religious courts. Uncertainty surrounding personal status regulations, especially in regard to marriage and divorce, had aroused the Coptic community. Both clergy and laity realized the threat to the integrity of the Coptic family from easy divorce and, ultimately, to the community. They wanted the door of conversion closed as an exit from Christian regulations and an entrance to Islamic legal advantages. It was an echo of Farid Antoun's plea at the 1953 meeting of the constitutional committee.

Frustrated in attempts to get a satisfactory hearing and assurances from the government, the bishops met on December 6, 1955, and proclaimed a "state of mourning" to be marked by a boycott of Christmas celebrations. This gesture of passive resistance was the ultimate weapon for a minority carrying on a dialogue of the deaf with the Moslem-dominated regime. It was a bold confrontation between Nasser and the Copts, a refusal to listen versus a demand to be heard. The bishops' proclamation stated:

> The Holy Synod has decided on the following:
> I) Proclamation of a state of mourning in all churches of the Mission of St. Mark, as follows: All churches will
>> a) ring their bells,
>> b) suppress all celebrations in their dioceses,
>> c) boycott all functions to which the church will be invited,
>> d) proclaim a fast at least until sunset and proclaim a time of prayer . . . refrain from making offerings or celebrating Mass on Wednesday, Thursday and Friday, January 4, 5, and 6, 1956.
> II) Close all churches in all dioceses Christmas Eve. On Christmas Day, January 7, prayers will be offered as usual.

III) Close the doors of the Patriarchate, the Bishoprics, the reception rooms of all churches on Christmas and refrain from exchanging greetings.

IV) If, despite these manifestations, no response is made to the demands of the Church and of the Holy Synod which stands by the Canons of the Church, each bishop will leave his Diocese and retire to a monastery in order to pray and to protest the attack upon a Sacrament of the Holy Church (Matrimony) until there is a favorable response to all their requests and the Church is once again placed in the hands of her priests: then prayers will be offered anew as is the custom on Sunday and Friday and at other times.

The Lord of the Church is powerful enough to preserve and protect her from all evil.

In seeking a conference with Nasser or one of his chief aides, the Copts had cooperated with other Christian groups in Egypt. In fact, the Catholics went ahead with their boycott, banning celebrations and midnight Mass on their Christmas preceding the Coptic Christmas. The most militant Catholic monsignor was jailed for five days in order to demonstrate the regime's annoyance and to break the monsignor's spirit.

As the Coptic Christmas approached, the Minister of Justice, the late Ahmed Hosny, agreed to a meeting with three bishops representing the Coptic Church and laymen representing the community. Even if Nasser regarded the Coptic minority as an annoying Egyptian fly, its buzz had become too loud. The planned gesture of defiance could have had repercussions at a time when the Nasser regime had not achieved its aura of invincibility, when intellectuals and businessmen were increasingly disgruntled about its encroachments, when Egypt's rivals in the Arab world were challenging Nasser's pretensions, and foreign interests were still strong in Egypt. It was the period before Suez, before crisis in Lebanon, revolution in Iraq and merger with Syria. Coincidentally, Marshal Tito was visiting Egypt, a leader hailed by the Coptic daily newspaper, "Misr," for his belief "that spiritual force is greater than material force," a convenient commendation that suited the circumstances in which the Copts found themselves. Though Tito has never been accused of being the pillar of any church, a Coptic protest was at least embarrassing to Nasser during those early days of his Tito courtship.

The Minister of Justice, who, ironically, had been accused of being a former Moslem Brother, was undoubtedly told to get the Copts to church on Christmas Eve. And he succeeded. The boycott was called off after his meeting with the Coptic committee. Said "Misr" in a compliant editorial addressed to Nasser: "We know of your solicitude for us; we have been calmed." Privately, the Copts have called that confrontation with the Minister of Justice "a Judas act . . . an errand run by fools . . . a crucial failure . . . a great betrayal."

At the meeting, Hosny apparently promised to satisfy the Coptic demands, especially by preventing divorce through conversion, so the Coptic committee announced that the Christmas boycott was unnecessary. Some Copts say that the bishops were satisfied by a promise that they would not lose their income from marriages and divorces and that their concern was more financial than theological. The bishop who had said, "I am a monk and have nothing to lose; I will not submit to the law," phoned Coptic bishoprics throughout the country calling off the boycott. Others say that Nasser's minister lied to the Coptic committee, that he had no intention of honoring their demands. Whether a misunderstanding or a deception, nothing was ever done about the Coptic objections and a turning point was reached in relations between the Copts and the Nasser regime. Their powers of defiance were considerably reduced and Nasser's ability to dominate the Copts was demonstrated. When Anba Yusab died the following fall—on November 14, 1956—the 23 members of the Community Council and 9 bishops unanimously elected Anba Asnathos, Bishop of Beni Suef, acting Patriarch. The Copts then faced the task of selecting a new Patriarch.

Wahda: Sign of unity at Alexandria's Railway Station.

Crossing the Nile near a Coptic village in Upper Egypt.

The Coptic Patriarch Kirillus VI at his installation.

The late Anba Yusab II, with servant and bodyguard, after
his banishment as Patriarch.

An early church fresco at the Coptic Museum.

Church of St. Mark at the
Coptic Patriarchate in
Cairo.

The entrance to the Coptic Museum.

Abuna Makari as-Suriani, the Patriarch's chief advisor, points to Coptic missionary areas in Africa while on a visit to the United States.

Coptic churchmen join in a welcome for Nasser on his return
from a trip abroad.

In the Monastery of al-
Muharraq near Assyut, a
monk prays.

Within a monastery in the Wadi Natrun, a monk stands by
his cell.

A view of the interior of the
Monastery of the Syrians
taken from the keep.

J.W.

The street of shops in the town of Akhmim where the famous
Coptic textiles are sold.

A Copt in Upper Egypt leaves his home under the sign of the
Cross over the doorway.

J.W.

CHAPTER XI

The Solitary Patriarch

At 10:20 a.m. on Sunday, April 19, 1959, Rafik Bassili al-
Toukhy, a five-year-old choir boy from the Nile Delta town
of Tanta, reached into an envelope containing three slips
of paper, each with the name of a different monk written on
it in India ink. The law of chance and a child's hand were
about to end several years of turmoil for the Copts by selecting a new Patriarch.

The throng crowding St. Mark's Church was understandably impatient. It was more than four years since the banishment of Patriarch Anba Yusab II, a painful and slow
amputation that was, in turn, followed by chaotic feuding
over the selection of a successor. The Coptic Mass on the
decisive Sunday had begun at 7:30 a.m. and had followed its
tireless course for almost three hours from chant to chant,
blessing to blessing. Outside it was spring in Cairo; inside,
clouds of incense still lingered in the air as the congregation
waited for the selection of "the Most Holy Pope and Patriarch of the great city of Alexandria and of all the land of
Egypt, of Jerusalem the Holy City, of Nubia, Abyssinia and
Pentapolis, and all the preaching of St. Mark."

News of the name chosen spread instantaneously through-

103

out Cairo; in less than an hour the monk's picture inscribed
with his new title was distributed on the streets. (Characteristically, some Copts who were later disappointed with the
choice were to comment on the promptness of the pictures.
Was the same name written on all three slips of paper?) At
the Church of St. Menas in Old Cairo, a servant began wildly
ringing the bells until he was stopped by Abuna Mina al-
Muttawahad al-Baramusi, who did not want to be interrupted
in the celebration of the Divine Liturgy. After the service,
this monk known as Mina al-Muttawahad (the Solitary)
made a simple comment on his selection as the new Patriarch: "This is a new test, a new task that God has given me."
Then he broke his fast with a cup of lemonade. Later, in a
statement directed more to His Maker than to his fellow
Copts, the Patriarch said: "I have always lived solitary, my
God, and I would have continued to live and die solitary.
But you have not wanted it. My God, may Your Will be
done, for Your Will is impenetrable and Your ways are mys-
terious, Lord."

Into the valley of Coptic confusion and discontent walked
the 116th Patriarch in the line leading back to St. Mark. A
saintly example of the revered monastic tradition, he ex-
alted his new role and humbled his personality, exhibiting
the proud humility which the faithful readily accept in the
dedicated solitary whose vision (and also viewpoint) belongs
to another world. The new Patriarch, called Kirillus VI,
even eclipsed the spectacle made by the Coptic Church and
community in selecting him. The grudging coalition of
bishops and laymen which brought about one Patriarch's
banishment had fallen apart when faced with selection of a
successor.

Should the Patriarch be chosen from the monks or the
bishops? Apparently an idle canonical question, but actually
a struggle for power, for control of land and money, and a
pursuit of the best means toward an end: Coptic survival.

The troubled times of the banished Patriarch exposed Coptic weakness, but at least the Copts demonstrated an ability to mobilize to meet the problem of banishment and of a Christmas boycott. Faced with the apparently straightforward matter of selecting a successor, their leadership declared bankruptcy. They could not unify to save themselves. "Perhaps," remarked the head of a distinguished Coptic family, "the Copts feud and squabble among themselves because they are not accustomed to self-rule. Also, they are accustomed to getting ahead by intrigue."

One week after the banished Patriarch's death, the Bishop of Beni Suef had been elected acting Patriarch, replacing the triumvirate of bishops who were administering the church; he supported the election of a monk as Patriarch. Within three months, the Coptic minority was in such turmoil over selection of candidates for Patriarch that the government intervened and stopped the election process on February 1, 1957. Though a representative of the Community Council asked the government to reconsider the decision, few could quarrel seriously with the announcement by the Ministry of Interior. Moslems and Copts read in their newspapers: "The Ministry found that there is a great deal of conflict between the Coptic community and the various religious circles around the office of Patriarch. The Ministry also found that the election campaign will be troublesome. Since the government is eager to preserve the dignity and holiness of the patriarchal church, to avoid bitter election campaigning and to ensure the selection of a candidate who will be a father and shepherd for all Christians, and since the country is facing certain circumstances [the after-effects of the Anglo-French-Israeli invasion of Suez], the Minister of Interior issued an order to stop the elections for Patriarch."

Lined up in confused battle positions in the overlapping territories of church and community, the Holy Synod and

the Community Council were at odds—loudly and publicly.
The Community Council, despite disagreements among its
members, appeared to favor a bishop for Patriarch. The
Holy Synod of bishops favored a monk. On December 9,
1956, the Holy Synod had announced in the wake of the
banished Patriarch's death that his successor must be over
40 years of age, with more than 15 years spent in a monastery. The bishops announced that they had decided not
to be candidates for Patriarch. Aware of the strong popular
feeling in favor of a monk and split into cliques, the bishops
wanted an outsider, a monk, to take over St. Mark's Chair.
Members of the Community Council, possibly with an eye
on four or five wealthy and ambitious bishops, looked forward to the naming of a cooperative Patriarch with a bishop's experience and qualifications.

Four days before the government's suspension of the election process, eight monks had presented themselves as candidates, including two whose names were eventually in the
decision-making envelope. One of the two was to become
Patriarch. By the day before the election was suspended, the
names of twenty-one monks and one bishop, Anba Mikhail
of Assyut, had been received.

Ideally, the pro-bishop argument is sound. The bishops,
who were themselves chosen from the monks, acquire administrative experience and worldly know-how. They have
a record which can be evaluated and the preparation needed
to assume the responsibilities of Patriarch. Even Mrs.
Butcher, who shunned criticism in her sympathetic history
of the Copts, argued against selection "of a saintly but ignorant monk from the Nitrian desert." She did so after
reporting, at the end of her two volumes, on the troubles
of Kirillus V, who was banished in 1883 following some
scandals. He returned to office "unwise and wasteful,"
though "honest and unselfish in the exercise of his trust." By
no means a new problem for the Coptic Church on its reap-

pearance in recent years, popular feeling and bad example tipped the scales in favor of a monk for Patriarch. The three Patriarchs prior to Kirillus VI had been chosen from the bishops and their reigns were regarded as disastrous for the church. A missionary summed up the feelings against selection of a bishop: "They were already corrupt." To the supplementary argument that the church should seek out well-educated leadership, Copts replied: "The Holy Ghost gives power and guidance to anyone chosen as Patriarch, even if he is not an intellectual."

One year later, in January 1958, the government permitted the election process to resume as the Copts became increasingly restive about the delay. (The wags in Cairo, mindful of the fact that Coptic clergy have long beards, were saying: "Nasser is waiting for one of his army officers to grow a beard that is long enough for a Patriarch.") The government in supporting the pro-monk feeling of the Holy Synod decreed that a candidate for Patriarch must be over 40 years of age, a monk for at least 15 years, "of good reputation and a holy man." Each bishop would name 12 electors for the patriarchal elections. They had to be men of good reputation and close to the church, who either had university degrees or paid over 100 pounds in taxes every year. That, in effect, confined the list of electors to the educated and the well-established. The bishops' list of electors had to be confirmed by the Community Council, which would take part in the voting, along with the bishops.

The election committee reflected the balance of power foreshadowed in the banishment of the Patriarch: three bishops, three members of the Community Council and an official from the Ministry of Interior. Church and community were given equal representation, but it was obvious that the government's one vote amounted to a potential veto. After the committee narrowed the monastic candidates to five, their names were placed on a ballot for the voting which would narrow the list to the three names in the decisive envelope.

On Sunday, April 12, 1959, special prayers in St. Mark's Church lasted from early morning until the afternoon and then a special three-day fast was announced by the church as 765 electors from Egypt, Jerusalem, Ethiopia and the Sudan gathered in Cairo. Minister of Supply Stino, who hovered over the proceedings as Nasser's man among the Copts, pleaded with his co-religionists to keep calm during the day-long voting. Each elector was given a card with the names of the final five on it. He could cross out two names and leave the three he favored for the final choice or he could cross out four names, thus giving a single choice his entire vote. Though the election was calm, it became obvious that the breach between community and church and between the pro-monk and pro-bishop groups remained. Twenty-two of the 24 members of the Community Council did not vote; neither did the bishops of Qena, Akhmim, Khartoum, Atbara, and Assyut (previously a patriarchal hopeful).

In the results announced April 17, 1959, the monk whose name was ultimately picked out of the envelope as Patriarch finished third in the balloting behind Damien al-Muharraq and Angelos al-Muharraq, two monks from the Monastery of al-Muharraq where the banished Patriarch spent his final months. Damien, who finished first, was made a bishop and assigned as Metropolitan of Atbara in the Sudan. Angelos, a small gentle monk who wept all day long while the voting went on, is tending in obscurity the meager and haphazard patriarchal library.

One evening, after the nightly liturgical service presided over by Kirillus VI with appropriate pomp and ceremony, the Patriarch's librarian showed off his library with child-like enthusiasm. A catalog was being drawn up for the collection. Copies of the Coptic daily newspaper, "Misr," and the Coptic weekly, "Watani," were stacked on a table. Some ancient manuscripts were behind glass doors, while miscellaneous volumes in Arabic and Coptic were visible on the shelves. In all, a modest parish for a monk whom the slip of a boy's hand could have made Patriarch.

At the time, that final step in choosing a Patriarch seemed archaic and absurd: the destiny of a church of four million decided in the 20th century by the blind law of chance. Yet on reflection, it shows an intuitive wisdom. In a minority torn by dissension and opposing ambitions, whose hierarchy and laity alternately compete and cooperate, a wide-open election for a single winner could be demoralizing. Electioneering and manipulation would have no bounds because of the high stakes involved for all Copts. By narrowing the contest to three and then tossing the decision to chance, the ambitious and the conniving are discouraged from mounting a destructive all-out campaign. The odds are two-to-one against them. Moreover, viewed religiously, the boy's hand only symbolically made the choice; God, as the newly-chosen Patriarch said, had chosen him. The prayer of consecration says, "He has become high priest, a shepherd and a teacher, since he has received the power from God."

On May 10, 1959, when Mina the Solitary was installed as Anba Kirillus VI, he wept throughout the ceremony, wiping his eyes with a colored handkerchief that he held in his left hand. In his right hand, he held a large Coptic gold cross. Copts reacted enthusiastically to the personification of sanctity rooted in their centuries-old tradition of monasticism. Dr. Otto Meinardus, a Protestant minister in Egypt who has become an expert on the Coptic Church, wrote: "A new era for the ancient Church of St. Mark may well have begun."

The new Patriarch went to the monastery cave where he had lived alone for four years and prayed and wept. When a bishop accompanying him, said, "God has chosen you," the Patriarch replied, "It's a great responsibility." Copts recalled a prophetic visit twenty years earlier by Patriarch

Anba Yuannis XIX to a monk living in a deserted windmill in Old Cairo. The aged Patriarch, leaning heavily on his patriarchal staff in the climb up the steep hill to the windmill, broke his staff. When the monk offered to repair it, the Patriarch insisted that Mina the Solitary—now the new Patriarch—keep the symbol of his office. The Copts relish such prophetic anecdotes; the divine origin of the choice is re-enforced.

Abuna Mina's life as a monk had begun at the age of 25 when he resigned from Thomas Cook's, the celebrated travel agency, after obtaining the Patriarch's personal permission to become a monk. While in secondary school in Alexandria, he had been inspired by reading the lives of famous monks; the monastery he selected was al-Baramus located near his birthplace in the Nile Delta village of Tukh an-Nasarah. Born in 1902, he was educated in a primary school in Damanhur, a predominantly Moslem town. Before joining Cook's in 1924, he worked with his brother in a Dutch firm.

As a young monk, he came under the influence of leading spiritual figures in the church; in middle age, he passed on inspiration to other young men, who are now part of a cadre of monks combining education and piety, rarely joined in the Coptic Church. Ordained in 1931, Abuna Mina attended the Helwan School for Monks for two years and, following a short stay in Upper Egypt, he entered a cave near the Monastery of al-Baramus. A famous monk at the monastery had been his spiritual father. A monk known as Abuna 'Abd al-Masih the Ethiopian and renowned as a prophet influenced Abuna Mina greatly as he lived his solitary life in the cave, going to the monastery only to obtain supplies of water and flour for baking his own bread. His harsh personal purification involved days of fasting and hours of prayer.

In 1936, after being refused permission to rebuild the Monastery of St. Menas near Alexandria, Abuna Mina moved to a deserted Napoleonic windmill in Old Cairo. He built his monastic cell and a small chapel, slept on the ground on sackcloth and lived off gifts of food. His growing fame as a mystic attracted Coptic pilgrims who came for his blessing. It was here that Patriarch Yuannis XIX made his prophetic visit.

According to Dr. Meinardus, the monk was expelled from the windmill during World War II by the British, who suspected him of spying. Another source maintains he was expelled to make room for archeological excavations. His prayerful message to the pious who surrounded him as he left his windmill characterizes his deep spiritual commitment: "Do not cry, my children. The Lord's Will must be done. His plans are sublime. The Lord will not abandon me. He who provides his feeding to the weakest bird will give me shelter and bread. Do not be anxious for me."

Abuna Mina stayed for a few years in a room near the Churches of St. Michael and St. Theodore the Eastern until his appointment in 1944 as head of the Monastery of St. Samuel in Upper Egypt. Though he was in the most isolated of the desert monasteries, pilgrims still traveled to Abuna Mina to obtain advice, prayers and blessing.

Next, he began his final pre-patriarchal phase by using the donations of pilgrims to build the Church of St. Menas in Old Cairo where he was praying on the day of his selection as Patriarch. In a settlement house adjacent to the church, he trained students for the monastic life; when this project was discontinued he rented rooms for a few piasters to university students from Upper Egypt. Of the present generation of monks who came under his influence two are outstanding: one is the vigorous and intelligent Abuna Makari as-Suriani, who is now his chief aide and advisor and the other is Abuna Matta al-Maskin, who periodically leaves his solitary cave to inspire university students and graduates engaged in a movement of spiritual revival.

In the first year of his reign as Patriarch, Kirillus VI de-

monstrated both his single-mindedness and his sense of the
religiously dramatic. Under his direction, two convoys of
cars—one from Cairo and one from Alexandria—converged
on a desert area where the Monastery of St. Menas once
stood. It was the monastery the Patriarch had tried to rebuild
a quarter of a century earlier in honor of his namesake,
Menas (or Mina), an Egyptian officer in the Roman Army
martyred in 296 A.D. for defiantly announcing his Christian
faith. The Patriarch had an altar set up on the reputed site
of the Menas tomb and, surrounded by crowds of Coptic
faithful and dignitaries who had traveled across the bumpy
and faceless Desert of Maryut, he celebrated the Divine
Liturgy. Then he went to the site of a monastery which will
be built so that monks—after a lapse of 1,000 years—will
once again inhabit the site of St. Menas. The inscription on
the foundation stone located so far from the daily life of
Egypt reads:

The Monastery of Abu Mina Thaumaturgus. Its foundation
stone was laid by the blessed hand of His Holiness, the Glorious
Pope Anba Kirillus VI, Pope of Alexandria and Patriarch of the
See of St. Mark, and this was on the blessed Friday, the 27th
of November, 1959, 17th of Hatur, 1676 A.M.

The new monastery, one of the first projects undertaken
by the Patriarch, occupied much of his attention. It involved
one of his first official contacts with the regime as he obtained
15 lonely desert acres for the monastery from the government's Department of Antiquities. In some ways, the incident
symbolizes the reign of the new Patriarch: religious grandeur
demonstrated by a charismatic leader suffering what the po-
litically-oriented regard as withdrawal symptoms. The community was besieged, the minority anxious, the hierarchy,
clergy and monks in disarray, the church wounded by turmoil, and the Patriarch lays a foundation stone in a deserted
place for another monastery.

Though the Patriarch's strength can be interpreted as the

community's weakness, he nonetheless reminded the Moslems indirectly that Egyptians were Christians long before they were Moslems and the Copts directly that they have a heritage of bravery and defiance of repressive authority. In personal contact, the Patriarch confirms what his gestures and words indicate. He is impregnable in his piety, unassailable on his spiritual mountain top. You talk and he hears, but he does not seem to listen or to belong to the present moment. The cross, the constant Coptic intermediary between man and God, seems to stand between the Patriarch and other humans. Ask him a question and he tends to answer with the sign of the cross as a blessing. Walking down the steps of the Patriarchate to greet the crowd that waits for him before the evening service, he makes the sign of the cross as he walks, stops so his gold cross can be kissed. Impervious, his expression still seems to be filled with the undistracted stare of the desert dweller.

From this spiritual height, he has surprised, stunned and chagrined the lackadaisical, the indifferent and the militant. He looks at the Copts and Egypt from a much different mountain top than does Nasser, and when the latter put pressure on the Patriarch for a ceremonial visit to the Presidency, he discovered the valley between them. It is said that the Patriarch replied to Nasser's indirect message that he should visit him: "The Patriarch is visited, but does not visit." After the Patriarch's election, Nasser sent a delegate to greet him and the Patriarch dispatched two bishops to return the gesture. When Nasser commented to the Coptic Minister, Stino, on the fact that the Patriarch didn't personally come to sign the presidential guest book, Stino carried the remark to the Patriarch, who replied: "Nasser sent one delegate. I sent two. He didn't elect me; God and Providence did." Then the Patriarch said to Stino: "Please don't try to take care of the church. It is my problem." Not until after several months of coolness did the Patriarch relent; on October 10, 1959, he visited the Presidential Palace and signed the guest book: "Best prayers, my true wishes and peace."

Within the church, the Patriarch has laid particular stress on rehabilitation of the religious life and observances. He made surprise visits to churches beginning at 5 a.m. and discovered that several parish priests were neglecting the early morning liturgy on Wednesdays and Sundays. When he found church doors closed that should have been open, he personally opened them and prayed inside. He struck out at the monks who were free-lancing as priests, ordering them back into the monasteries away from worldly distractions. To the monks who were scandalizing the faithful by collecting money indiscriminately, he issued a firm order: get the Patriarch's personal permission before doing any collecting.

When the See of Guergueh, where his predecessor had been archbishop, became vacant, he stunned the leading Coptic family in that area by depriving them of their usual prerogative of picking the bishop. In a miniature patriarchal ceremony, the head of the family had called a public meeting at which he put the names of three monks in a box and selected one of them as the next bishop. Since all the local clergy were under the family's thumb, any winner would suit the family. Soon after, the family head died, and his family visited the Patriarch to tell him of their choice for bishop. When the Patriarch demurred, the family threatened: "We will convert to Catholicism unless you take our man." They had miscalculated by invading the Patriarch's spiritual territory and he raised his voice: "No, No, No." The Patriarch left the see open for some time and then appointed his own choice.

As Anba Kirillus' personal sanctity inspired Copts throughout Egypt, he toured the country and received enthusiastic receptions by crowds everywhere. This ability to summon strong responses from the Coptic faithful is undoubtedly his strongest weapon in dealing with the Nasser regime. The natural inclination of the Copts, and indeed all

Egyptians, is toward loyalty for a strong, dedicated individual and on this score Anba Kirillus has had an unparalleled success as a religious leader among the Coptic Patriarchs of this century.

By piety and performance, the Patriarch touches the emotional, high-strung religious feelings of the Copts. He wakes daily at 3 a.m. to pray; he officiates publicly at the daily celebrations of the liturgy. During Lent, he fasts daily from midnight to 6 p.m. when he celebrates Lenten Mass. When the press interviewed him after his installation, he answered difficult questions with the admonition: "It is better not to speak, rather to pray."

Copts everywhere showed awareness of his sanctity. A writer said: "The Patriarch is very popular because he is a simple and pious man and consoles everyone. He prays long hours. He is not an ambitious man, the idea of actually being Patriarch was only a dream to him." An archeologist: "The Patriarch has prestige. He is a man of peace, of love and of faith." An editor: "The Patriarch is well-liked . . . he prays very much." An engineer: "He is well-liked as holy . . . he is also popular for his tours among the people."

According to the canons of the Coptic Church, the Patriarch directs the church in collaboration with the bishops. He is Bishop of Alexandria, the first bishop, the senior bishop, but the actual title Patriarch is not used in the church canons. He does not claim infallibility and his functions are equivalent to those of the other bishops, except that the right of installing bishops belongs exclusively to him. In practice, of course, he is the pope of the Egyptian Christians, a role shaped by its holder. Therefore, his own view of the role and his policies are necessary to any description of the Coptic Church.

In collaboration with his chief advisor and aide, Abuna Makari as-Suriani, a series of written questions were presented to the Patriarch. Abuna Makari discussed the answers with the Patriarch and framed the answers on his behalf. Since Abuna Makari is intimately involved in policy making for the Patriarch, any merging of the viewpoints of the two men re-enforces the validity of the answers. The following summary of answers in the third person underlines the spiritual emphasis of Anba Kirillus and his concentration on the Copts as a religious community:

What is your great ambition for the Coptic Church during your reign as Patriarch? His great ambition is to see the church in a spiritual revival that resembles the early days of the Apostolic Fathers. As a hermit, he has had very deep experience with prayer and a great faith that prayer will lead the church to this great revival. He is trying to encourage all Coptic congregations to develop this experience with prayer. He feels prayers have solved the three major problems of the church:

1. The Ethiopian problem. (An agreement was signed June 25, 1959, removing points of friction between the Coptic Churches of Egypt and Ethiopia) .

2. Unity: Before the selection of the present Patriarch, the people were "eating" each other. Now all are behind the Patriarch.

3. Waqfs: For 70 years, the waqfs (religious endowments) were a stumbling block in the life of the church and now they have been reorganized.

Prayer did all this, without the necessity of speaking about it. The rest of our problems will be solved this way.

What is the church's greatest need? Spiritual revival and social unity.

Does the Patriarch plan to hold any discussions with the government? We are always in touch with the government whenever necessary. Stino [Coptic Minister of Supply] is the government's liaison officer on Coptic matters. We send him most of our petitions and he sends them to the President. Sometimes we contact Nasser directly or the government ministers concerned. Most of the time we receive favorable responses and good will.

What is the prayer of the Patriarch for Christianity in the world? He is praying for Christians to be real Christians and to have a spiritual revival everywhere. In the Coptic liturgy there is a litany in which we repeat the prayer that God will help the churches to end disunity.

Though the religious uplift is inspiring, the Coptic militants are dissatisfied with the de-emphasis of the temporal, the political and the practical in the reign of the new Patriarch. A priest still determined to fight the Coptic battle complained: "The Patriarch is a very holy man; he is a saint. So is his assistant, Father Makari, and he is also very intelligent and well-educated. There is much praying every day at the Patriarchate, but we need more than prayer. Prayer is not enough."

Daily reminders of Coptic anxiety pour into the Patriarchate by mail and personal visits. The number is alarming, and though church officials are sensitive about discussing them, there is little doubt that their recurring themes reflect the main motives for converting to Islam: the advantage of easy divorce by conversion, the lure of jobs, the hope of economic advantage, the avoidance of discrimination and Moslem pressures.

While the Patriarch tends to see his role primarily in religious terms, he is also the head of the community and "politics is part of his job," according to a prominent Coptic lawyer. Those who are disappointed with the Patriarch argue that the reminders of Coptic anxiety require more attention to the temporal and an enlarged definition of prayer. The Pope in Rome and the Archbishop of Canterbury do the Lord's work at their desk as well as the altar.

Unfortunately for this viewpoint, the church's image of a holy man is not of a man of action—unlike the Moslem view which celebrates as its greatest prophet Mohammed, a man of sword and sermon. The present Patriarch, Kirillus VI, whose entire life has been dedicated to a kingdom not of this world, continues to be absorbed in prayer and contemplation and is not easily distracted from this absorption. Not only has a monk become Patriarch, but the Patriarch has remained a monk.

CHAPTER XII
Children of the Desert

The Coptic monks of Egypt are men who have found eternal meaning in life and have taken their simple certitude into the unchanging environment of the Egyptian desert where it will not be disturbed. They have been there since the father of monasticism, St. Anthony, began his pursuit of solitude in third-century Egypt, though the notion of dwelling apart goes back to sanctuaries set aside in the temples of ancient Egypt and to lodgings for pagan priests in isolated tombs.

The desert is the overwhelming reality in the environment. Its timeless sand, inhospitable empty horizon and cloudless sky with its abrupt sunsets are interrupted only by passing camels or occasional palm trees that look like sentries remaining at their posts after the army has moved on. At noon, the sunlight is hypnotic and at night, the emptiness envelops and pacifies. One evening as we left a monastery, the crescent moon cast a pale light over the desolate surroundings as we started to tramp through the sand to our jeep about two miles away. The abbot at the monastery door took a last look around and said what all of us were thinking: "The desert stillness is captivating."

Monasticism in Egypt is that simple: eternal verities protected by a compelling, unchanging environment. The monks can alter the desert only slightly: some cultivated acreage, monastery buildings surrounded by walls, the sound of a bell, the chant of the liturgy. The desert has made the terms of the bargain and in exchange it renders the pious monk impregnable, as it has the monk-Patriarch, Kirillus VI.

When Anthony heard his Gospel message, "If thou wilt be perfect, sell all thou hast and give to the poor . . . and come follow me," he responded with a literalness that still characterizes Coptic monks. He rid himself of his 300 inherited acres and began his life of dwelling apart. Eventually he responded to pleas of disciples for guidance in the life of solitude which he came to exemplify for his own and all succeeding generations.

This ran parallel to the example of a contemporary, Paul of Thebes, who is regarded as the first hermit. Whereas other people in other places fled persecution by going into a mountain fastness—as in the Lebanon—the Egyptian Christians had only the desert and so it was that Paul fled the third-century persecution of the Emperor Decius. Paul remained in solitude until the meeting between him and Anthony that is celebrated in medieval art. Paul is said to have asked Anthony: "Yet because love endureth all things, tell me, I pray thee, how fares the human race? Have new roofs risen in the ancient cities? Whose empire is it that now sways the world? And do any still survive snared in the error of the demons?" Both the tradition of Paul the Hermit and Anthony the Monk continue side by side in Egypt; while all modern Egyptian monks are attached to monasteries, some go apart into caves to live in solitude.

Both methods and mood have changed as little as the desert. Primitive monasticism is consciously preserved in pursuit of the "angelic life" in the eight active Coptic monasteries in Egypt. It is a passive life, avoiding teaching, special studies, or any of the activities associated with Western monasticism. The monks, remaining celibate unlike Coptic priests, perform the Divine Office each day, fast, and do penance, concentrating on explicit acts of worship.

To quote two of Anthony's characteristic third-century admonitions is to summarize his echo in the stated attitudes of twentieth-century Coptic monks:

Short indeed is man's life if set beside the ages to come and all our time is nothing compared to eternal life. In the world everything is sold for what it is worth, and a thing is exchanged for another of equal value. But the promise of eternal life is cheaply bought. . . . Let us not look back upon the world and fancy we have given up great things. For the whole earth is a very little thing compared with the whole of Heaven.

At the Monastery of St. Anthony, revered as the saint's final resting place, the monks make a point of paying personal homage to Anthony each time they enter the monastery church. Otherwise, they report, the saint will personally remind them of their omission. Dr. Otto Meinardus, in his study of the Coptic monasteries, reports the story told by one monk who was sent to fetch a book from the church. In his haste, he neglected to pay his respects to Anthony. Suddenly, the monk appeared outside the church, pale and trembling, reporting that St. Anthony had tapped him on the shoulder. Other monks at the monastery also say they have felt or seen St. Anthony.

This is typical of the unreserved faith of the monks who are surrounded by pious coincidences that are accepted as unmistakable testimonials and reassuring omens. In setting the religious style, tone and ideals of the church, the monks have a profound influence over the Coptic position as a minority. Each group of people draws on folk heroes and prototypes, usually men of action with pen, sword or proselytizing tongue. The Copts draw on these passive holy men

who escape the aura of venality that surrounds Coptic laymen or bishops seeking power. But their perspective makes
monks unlikely men of action. Their inspiration is like the
hashish used by Egyptian peasants; they pacify and weaken
the will to act. Leaders recruited from pious monks are likely
to resemble the present monk-Patriarich and the men he has
chosen to assist him. An unshakable confidence that even
passive faith guarantees ultimate victory may inspire monks
but it also paralyzes the community of Copts.

Those Copts who rely on the monks accept in effect the
prophecies attributed to a tenth-century sanctuary door in
the church of the Monastery of the Syrians. Its seven rows of
panels are seriously regarded by the monks as the way of the
past, present and future. What the visitor sees and the monks
decipher runs as follows: First row—figures of Christ,
Blessed Virgin, St. Mark, St. Ignatius of Antioch, St.
Dioscorus and St. Severus (the Apostolic Age); Second row—
pattern of circles interlaced to form crosses (expansion of
Christianity); Third row—linked circles containing crosses
(formation of episcopal sees of early church); Fourth row
—series of crosses encircled by four-leaf shamrocks (rise of
Islam as it encircled Christianity); Fifth row—swastikas
within circles (rise of materialism, including Nazism); Sixth
row—a mixture of a dark grill, white areas and linked
circles (weakness of the church); Seventh row—a plain cross
filling each of six panels (unity and ultimate triumph of
the church).

Inside that dimly-lit church in the middle of the desert
at Wadi Natrun—halfway between Cairo and Alexandria—
this post-facto prophecy explained in a pious whisper by a
monk holding a candle to the panels is well-protected. There
is the strength of Coptic monasticism behind it: all-en-
veloping faith, insulation, ultimate confidence. Defects too:
inflexibility, naïveté, too much sense of history, too little
historic sense. These monastic children of the desert are not

made to sustain their fellow Copts in the modern social, economic and political pressures they face. It is too much to ask of 400 monks by four million Copts.

In terms of the church itself, three youthful monks have particular impact. Two of them confirm the pattern and are usually found in desert caves. The other is the most important of the Patriarch's three aides, Abuna Makari as-Suriani, who acted as the Patriarch's spokesman in answering my questions. He is usually referred to as "the intelligent one at the Patriarchate. He went to Princeton." Besides his master's degree from Princeton Theological Seminary, Abuna Makari received a law degree from the University of Cairo and a liberal arts degree from the American University at Cairo. He also taught at the Coptic seminary in Ethiopia.

Abuna Makari is an exception. He is the only member of the monastic elite who is addressing himself to the contemporary problems facing the Copts and he gives the impression that he is an able tactician. As the church's traveling representative to ecumenical meetings and Christian conferences all over the world, he is also the main conductor of Western church influences. His Princeton experience has impressed him and he is proud of his master's thesis which, upon reading, turns out to be a solid, workmanlike summary of the church, though not much of a blueprint for action or for significant analysis. Nonetheless, Abuna Makari is trying to find solutions, though his critics point out there is little evidence of achievement and some signs of patriarchal ambitions.

The second influential monk, Abuna Matta al-Maskin, led the third, Abuna Antunius as-Suriani, and ten other young monks into desert caves in the way of St. Anthony. Abuna Matta's statement of intent illustrates the durability of the Antonian tradition:

"Christianity can be revived only by a revivification of the genuine monastic ideal, which is the life and the teaching of

our fathers . . . here [in the desert] we are poor, poor like our
fathers, we have no library, yet our books are written in our
minds to serve our minds . . . and in religion, which is the life
with God, the true philosophy comes from the heart to serve
the heart; thus we don't need a library, our library is within
us, our hearts contain the library of God."

A university graduate in pharmacology, Abuna Matta had
turned his back on the world by selling his pharmacy in the
Nile Delta town of Damanhur—a lucrative business that
attracts many Copts. He joined the most isolated Coptic
monastery, St. Samuel in Upper Egypt, which is separated
by about 40 miles from the nearest mud village, and then
sought further solitude for three years in a cave. He left
temporarily for an assignment as a patriarchal vicar in
Alexandria, where he developed a following among university students and teachers. When he returned to monastic
solitude, he gathered his band of eleven, many of them
university men, and went to desert caves near the Monastery
of St. Samuel.

Abuna Antunius, who is a graduate of Cairo University,
eventually left the group and returned to a cave near the
Monastery of the Syrians to which he belongs, interrupting
his solitude only to carry on the duties of librarian for the
monastery. The present Patriarch persuaded him to serve as
a patriarchal secretary, but he remained only three months.
In that time, he never left his room except to perform his
duties.

The cave now inhabited by Abuna Antunius was cut in
ancient times into the lifeless sandstone that forms ridges in
the desert. It is twelve feet long and three feet high and
wide, providing barely enough room for a bed of sandstone,
a small desk, crude kitchen facilities, a mat and various
religious books and commentaries. It is the meaningful uni-
verse of this monk who is regarded as a leading theologian
of the Coptic Church.

Throughout the church's history the vigor and discipline of the monastic life has measured the condition of the church; they thrived or declined together. It is a close relationship linked from the very beginning of the church's independence when monks led the reaction against condemnation of Monophysitism by the Council of Chalcedon in 451 A.D. The growth of monasticism and asceticism in a country which has been described as "one vast monastery" earned for Egypt at that time the title of "Holy Land" in preference to Palestine. But not all the monks were gentle, for they were also known in those days for their fanaticism. They led mobs in Lower Egypt that destroyed pagan temples and they laid lusty and destructive hands on the mammoth monuments of Pharaonic Egypt.

Though the monks had periods in which they flourished after the Moslem conquest of Egypt (at one point, the caliphs spent their summer holidays in Christian monasteries), they were subject to murderous attacks and the monasteries had by this time become religious fortresses with towers of refuge in case of attack. The famous Wadi Natrun monasteries, in particular, had always been subject to the attacks of desert tribesmen. After each attack, the monks who survived re-established their monastic routine. Of the seven important monasteries that once existed in Wadi Natrun, four remain.

Of the four, the Monastery of the Syrians is the outstanding example of modern monasticism in Egypt and was particularly praised by the present Patriarch during his tour of monasteries in the fall of 1961. It was also praised by a Western Trappist who stayed there during a tour of Egypt. A visit to the monastery confirms this favorable impression. According to tradition, the monastery, whose formal name is the Monastery of the Holy Virgin and St. John Kame, is built on the model of Noah's Ark. Its tower, once used as a refuge in case of attack, looks out over the main church of the Virgin and three smaller churches. St. Ephrem's Tree, a striking tamarind tree seven feet in diameter, is regarded as the offspring of a staff stuck into the ground by the saint in the fourth century. In its modern resurgence, the monastery has added a library, museum, press, water tower and retreat house.

The latter houses young men who come, as one explained, "to rest and to build up strength to face the world." They come singly, in pairs or sometimes three at a time, taking a bus to the rest house on the Cairo-Alexandria highway and then walking three hours across the desert to the monastery. The abbot explained, "Anyone who knocks and has a good face, we welcome him."

These pious guests are personal conductors to the outside world of the monastic influence; they follow the holy men to their places as Egyptians always have and return to the cities and towns to give testament. In their monastery stay, they have maximum contact with the monks and become temporary disciples.

A university student staying at the monastery described the layman's daily routine:

4 a.m.—Communal prayer

5 to 7:30 a.m.—Mass

7:30 to 8:30 a.m.—Breakfast

8:30 to 10:30 a.m.—Keep silence and meditate

10:30 to 2:00 p.m.—Work around the monastery, read or meditate

2:00 to 4:30 p.m.—Lunch and rest

4:30 to 5:00 p.m.—Wash and prepare to resume spiritual activity

5:00 to 5:30—Communal prayer

5:30 to 8:00—Reading, work and conferences with the monks who "talk to us about our lives and our sins and about the future"

8:00 to 8:30—Supper

8:30 to 10:00—More meetings with monks, individually and in groups

The schedule reflects the Coptic appetite for the ascetic life. Even university students who leave Cairo and Alexandria for a desert retreat feel the routine is suitable; they regard it as a major part of their heritage. As expressed by a prominent Coptic archeologist: "We Copts all have the microbe of the faith, of abstinence, of monasticism. I myself could sell everything and be satisfied. Our period of fasting is coming and I am very glad." Indeed, fasts recur throughout the Coptic year. Besides a seven-week Lenten fast, the church prescribes 43 days of fasting before Christmas, 15 days before the Feast of the Assumption of the Mother of God, 15 to 49 days before the Feast of the Apostles Peter and Paul, depending on the date of Easter. Also the one-week fast of Heraclius and the three-day fast of Jonah. When Copts fast, they abstain from meat, eggs, milk, butter and cheese. During the Assumption, Jonah and Lenten fasts, they abstain completely from food and drink until midday.

The unquestioning acceptance of their monasticism by most Copts prompts the practical observation that it tends to squander ideals, energies and youthful dedication. In times of stress, the anchorite is a community luxury, mortgaging the present for the future. Basically, his act is self-centered; while it inspires many, it serves as a realistic model for very few. Kept in its primitive state, monasticism not only has made few contributions to the community of Copts, but its built-in passivity even runs downhill into religious laxity. A simple bearded man in black robes and sandals, the monk often has become an empty anachronism, doing little, praying little and losing himself in a personal nirvana. His condition has generally declined under the lax central rule of the church during most of this century, and the monk has turned up as a bedraggled beggar in the midst of urban poverty or as a religious functionary hiring himself out to Coptic parishes. When the Patriarch ordered the monks back to the monasteries, half of them were outside monas-

tery walls. Hinting at a Western influence that represents
more of a wish than a realistic goal, the Patriarch announced: "The monasteries will become once more religious
schools where monks will devote time to study and writing."

One publicized example of monastic decline has been
feuding within monastery walls. When such trouble makes
newspaper headlines, including the world press, it tends to
justify Moslem scorn for the religious quality of the Coptic
religion. For instance, the Monastery of al-Muharraq (the
Virgin Mary), located near the Coptic center of Assyut,
has had repeated uprisings against the authority of its
bishop. In 1936, 1937, 1939, 1947 and as recently as April
1959, the monks rose in protest and locked out their bishop
in defiance of both civil and church authority.

The venal side of life in Egypt has not left the monks in
peace either. Some monasteries have considerable wealth,
represented by fertile acreage bequeathed to them as waqfs
(religious endowments). It has been enough to turn the heads
of some bishops and to cause bitter community strife. In
1950, when a dedicated Copt singlehandedly put together a
general guide on the Copts—the only one of its kind—he
had to use an accounting made in 1941. His explanation
speaks for itself: "We wish we could publish the current
[monastery] budget but it is unknown and is in the hands
of the head of each monastery."

Some monastery lands have been treated as the personal
real estate holdings of the supervising bishops and abbots.
Not surprisingly, the strife-ridden Monastery of al-Muharraq, located where the Copts have always been most powerful and most able to bequeath land, is the wealthiest, with
2,800 acres. The second wealthiest is the Monastery of St.
Anthony, with 1,200 acres. The abbot of St. Anthony had to
be forcibly removed in 1960 and replaced by a new abbot
"known for his holiness and his solicitude for church properties." The deposed abbot was then confined to the poorest

monastery, Anba Bishoi in Wadi Natrun; it only has about 100 acres. The total of the monastery holdings amounts to 5,300 valuable acres.

Nonetheless, the potential of the monastic movement remains, for the Coptic community as well as the church. Modernization is an obvious possibility, but there is also the ability of the saintly monk to capture the imagination of the Copts. The Patriarch Kirillus VI has demonstrated this. Such a monk could also mobilize the Copts and galvanize them into action. Standing above corruption, the saintly monk is indifferent to punishment, for no jail cell matches the severity of a desert cave and death holds no terror for those who regard life as a passing fancy.

What is necessary is transformation of the single-minded other-world commitment to concern about modern problems. Imminent danger to the Coptic religion could act as a catalyst for such a transformation and produce a monk in heroic dress who defies the Moslem majority, the regime and the multiplying pressures against the minority. Such a man would shatter the monastic mold and transfer his heavenly gaze to earthly problems. It would be a martyr's gesture, not in the latter-day version of a believer who is done in but in the crusading version of the martyr who dies fighting. It is the difference between the passive and the active commitment and like all things in Egypt it has a precedent, in this instance the militant monks of the early church. Somewhere in a lonely cave the desert alchemy could make a monk messianic and it could happen at any time.

CHAPTER XIII

The People's Church

The Coptic Church is probably the only Christian church whose laity in the twentieth century has been more dedicated than its clergy. The church's survival depends more on the commitment of its parishioners than on the work or the example of its priests. Throughout Egypt, most of the congregation is still waiting for its priests to provide spiritual leadership and to re-enforce their identity as Copts.

While a Copt is more than a member of the church—even atheists remain Copts—the church is needed to put a Coptic seal on the beginning (baptism), the middle (marriage) and the ending (burial) of each life story. As the instrument for these ritual acts, which have either symbolic or spiritual meaning for Copts, or both, the priest is surrounded with such respect that Copts still kiss his hand on greeting him. Yet the respect usually has more symbolism than personal esteem in it. Middle and upper class Copts regard priests as social inferiors. Educated Copts are openly disdainful.

A Coptic sociologist voiced a prevalent attitude: "Coptic priests are ignorant, even in religious matters. I have never met a Coptic priest who has attracted me to the affairs of the

130

spirit." An intellectual from Assyut, though a highly committed Copt, dismissed the clergy with the estimate that there are only about seven "good priests" in Egypt. The priests, who marry before ordination, are regarded as more concerned with their families than with their churches. The complaints are repetitious; in the beginning of this century when there were about 700 Coptic priests, a Western commentator wrote: "If one applies for information to the Coptic clergy, one is met either by economy of fact, which is more misleading than silence, or by genuine ignorance."

Dr. Wahib Attulah, head of the Coptic Seminary and the leading authority on the clergy, placed the number of "good" priests—that is, performing their duties adequately—at 200. He made it clear that the rest are either incompetent or indifferent. It is also obvious that the Coptic Church doesn't know exactly how many priests it does have. Dr. Attulah says there are about 700 Coptic priests; other figures cited are 800 and 1,000 for about 700 churches. Not surprisingly, the Coptic Patriarchate makes the highest estimate—1,100 priests.

By any of the rough counts, there are not enough Coptic priests to sustain such a large membership unless the people want their Coptic Church to survive. The observation is strengthened by the acknowledged low quality of the clergy, who generally have been selected and trained haphazardly, then ordained by a mixed lot of bishops individually exercising their power to ordain. Overnight ordinations have been common throughout Egypt; one day an engineer or pharmacist, the next a priest. Coptic congregations selected a candidate for the priesthood, thereby asserting their vested interest in the priest as a symbol, and the choice was usually a respected and pious man who helped out in church. The local bishop promptly ordained him. He was married or got married before ordination, since the Copts feel that parish priests, who visit homes and hear women's confessions, must be married. Priests cannot marry after ordination. Monks who assisted in parish work never made house calls and if they heard confessions, it was only of men. Like all Middle Easterners, the Copts are concerned about the proprieties and worried about the care and protection of sexual virtue.

In the summer of 1960, the Patriarch ruled that all candidates for the priesthood must be graduates of the Coptic Seminary and that exceptions require his special approval. A professor at the seminary, who bemoaned the fact that the bishops were ordaining priests with no knowledge of theology, stressed the importance of this ruling. But there still is a long distance in Egypt from the Patriarch's lips to the local bishops' ears.

The role of the congregation in sudden ordinations was illustrated a few months before the Patriarch's order when the Copts in a Nile Delta town rebelled against their elderly parish priest. He had antagonized them by turning down a local manufacturer's offer to build a second Coptic church in the town. Afraid of competition, the priest asked, instead, for money to repair his own church. The town's Copts banded together, collected money for a new church and selected a government worker as their priest. He left his job at 9 o'clock in the morning and was a priest before lunch. Fortunately, in this instance, the choice was devout and competent and also willing to reduce his salary by two-thirds in order to become a priest. He had served an informal apprenticeship as a deacon for many years, learning church procedures and liturgy.

For the most part, priests and monks have been recruited from the lower classes. No family with any financial means or standing considers the priesthood suitable, even for its black sheep. A vicious circle re-enforces itself: because the clergy has little esteem, it has attracted recruits of low quality and this in turn perpetuated the low esteem. Just as Egyptians under Nasser came under the rule of the products of a military system they despised, the church of the Copts is largely in the hands of the community leftovers. Those with talent and social status went into the traditional Coptic activities in business and the professions. To a large extent, the church got second-rate people, proceeded to neglect their training, paid them low salaries and burdened them with a variety of duties. The priests, in turn, added to their personal burdens by producing large families.

For instance, one Cairo priest described his duties as follows: teach theology at the Coptic Seminary, carry on parish duties in the most heavily populated area in Cairo and raise a family of three boys and three girls. His priestly duties include a time-consuming liturgy, marriages, funerals, baptisms, confessions, and visits to parishioners. In the Middle East where the lackadaisical ways of the Levant replace the exertions of the Protestant ethic, one can only speculate on the quality of his theological scholarship and the intensity of his parish activities. Of his traditional devotion to family, there can be no doubt. It also means that he is not likely to be very bold or outspoken, for his children need government jobs and scholarships and he needs his modest salary. Clearly, he has too many hostages to fortune.

The relationship between Coptic priest and people was characterized by a sympathetic observer, an Egyptian Catholic priest who has spent his career in welfare work among Copts in Cairo. "The Coptic people are more attached to their religion than are their clergy, which is opposite to the situation in the Western church," he said. "For many members of the Coptic clergy, it's a job, something like law or medicine, except that it doesn't require as much intellectual effort while appealing to the Oriental pleasure in sitting back and being important. There is a kind of complicity between the people and the clergy. The people accept the priest as a leader who helps them feel secure as a member of the group. As in an army, they have their local officers nearby who are their contact with the large army. The Copts are sensitive about their position as a minority surrounded by Moslems, but when they fill the church together, they feel protected."

The unifying function of the church is particularly evident at Sunday Mass. In their animated celebration of the changing of bread and wine into the divinity of Christ, the Copts fill the church with the tangibles of religious worship. Sight, sound, smell, touch are all involved as the congregation acts out membership in the group. The mood of the Christian East takes over almost immediately, and for the outsider the note is struck at the memorable moment when the cymbals clash for the first time and the handful of deacons at the altar explode into the Coptic chant. It is an exotic sing-song that wails and shouts in fits and starts; its style has been traced to the temple music of the Pharaohs. Repeatedly, the priest adds his solo chant and assaults the air with heavy clouds of incense so that the drowsy, sticky aroma never leaves the church during a service lasting more than two hours. (The Copts, consistently traditional, are proud of their "uncut, unchanged" version of the Mass.)

On entering the church each worshipper leaves a small donation in exchange for a loaf of "holy bread," shaped like an eight-inch loaf of French bread. Then men and women go to separate sections, fathers clutching sons who frequently munch on their bread during the Mass, and mothers holding daughters, including the serious little girl who stuffs her holy bread into a tiny pocketbook. The mood is domestic, though a sense of excitement is generated by the explosions of Coptic chant, the shaking of incense, the sound of cymbals, hand bells and triangles, and the bowing en masse as the praises of the Lord are sung. It is action worship.

The church usually has only a handful in attendance when the Mass begins and fills up steadily until the final stragglers, arriving a few minutes before the end, stand huddled in the

rear. It is as if the ceremony began unannounced, and
passersby, attracted by the commotion, joined their neighbors
to form a large crowd. My companion at one such Mass in
the fashionable Cairo suburb of Heliopolis claimed that the
late arrivals are a ways the best dressed; apparently, lateness
is directly proportional to social standing.

According to a Westerner who has observed the Copts in
the rural areas, they go to church as to a village affair. "In
church," she added, "they listen . . . to the chanting, the
reading of the Scriptures. They don't seem to understand
the Mass, but they feel that the longer the church service the
more efficacious."

A strategic gesture of unity takes place at Mass when the
"blessing is passed around," a chain reaction of physical
contact that binds the entire congregation. This occurs after
the sermon as each Copt clasps his neighbor's hands, to the
right and left, front and rear.

Unmistakably, the weekly Mass is a rallying place for the
Copts, where they reaffirm their identity and their membership in the group. In such ways, the Church of Egypt is made
custodian of their ancient identity. Though they need such
a custodian, use and maintain it, the Copts still regard it
primarily as their servant, not as their master. And though
they readily respect the priest as a symbol, they are quick
to criticize him as a person and slow to follow him as a leader.

While their identity is tied to the Coptic Church, the pas-
sionate piety of the Copts is unreservedly committed to the
message of Christ and the meaning of the Cross. If the Coptic
hurch and its priests are not there to provide religious outlets (and often they are not), Copts turn to the Franciscan
missionary or the American Presbyterian. They maintain
Coptic allegiance and often continue to use the Coptic
church for baptism and marriage. But they will go to the
Presbyterian or Catholic church on Sundays, attend their
prayer meetings, use their welfare centers and send the

children to their schools. The personal faith of the Copts is
usually so amorphous, once you go beyond Christ and the
Cross, that it can accommodate any Christian church.

Doctrinal niceties are not a strong point even with the
Coptic clergy, and when you reach deeply into rural Egypt
you find what a Catholic missionary sister found in Koussieh,
a town 200 miles south of Cairo. The Coptic women who
flock to Catholic catechism classes and services feel that there
is no reason to convert. The French-speaking nun, undaunted
but realistic, reported that they feel it is "la même chose."
Some say they would like to become Catholics when they are
dying, but meanwhile they don't call themselves either Copts
or Catholics. They are Christians and they point to the
crosses tattooed on their wrists.

The religious intensity of the Copts is greatest in Upper
Egypt where life is harshest and filled with cruel and fickle
tragedy. Their faith is repeatedly described as "child-like"
and it is not surprising. For the Egyptian peasant, chained
to the land and its pitiful rewards, life can hardly be coped
with or even endured. Only the Nile's regular flooding
saves him from starvation. It is a lot shared by Moslem and
Copt, but the latter also faces the hostility of the Moslem
environment.

The cross suits this cruel culture of poverty and persecution, both an identification and an outlet for the Copts.
It is their brand and their balm; it gives a meaning to life
when there are only blind nature and inexplicable misfortune. If Western Christianity gives prime glory to Easter—
the day of Resurrection, deliverance and confirmation of
Christ's divinity—Good Friday is more appropriate psychologically to the Copts. On this day when the cross was born as
a universal Christian symbol, modern Copts say "Kyrie
eleison" (Lord, have mercy upon us) 400 times at home,
100 times in each direction, and flock to their churches. At
Easter time, Copts make the traditional pilgrimage to Jeru-

salem and return with ornate crosses tattooed on their arms.

A member of a prominent Coptic family in Cairo described a characteristic example of religious involvement.
His grandfather, a wealthy man, established a family custom
of feeding the worshippers in several churches so they could
remain as long as possible in church from Holy Thursday
until Easter midnight Mass. Each of the sons, including his
father, carried on the custom in one of the churches so that
he can recall staying at church as a child from Holy Thursday to Saturday night, even sleeping there with his family.
The money for Holy Week feeding, which comes from bonds,
must be supplemented nowadays so that the custom can continue. The prominent engineer who still maintains this
family custom was emphatic on his own religious attitude:
"I don't go to church myself. I feel the Copts are more a race
than a religion." But Good Friday is the exception; he always goes to church on that day. Why? "I have to go."

While the Copts share the cross with the rest of Christianity, with no other group is its presence so obsessive. This
ranges from the Patriarch, who holds the cross in front of
himself as though it were both a shield and a weapon, to the
ragged village children who run after strangers, crude blue
tattoos of the cross on the inside of their right wrists and
crosses around their necks. Whenever the Patriarch appears,
Copts rush forward to kiss his cross; after evening prayer
services they line up to kiss the cross. The fixation is symbolized at baptism when the infant is anointed 36 times all
over his body.

Crosses are painted over the doors of Coptic houses in
towns and villages or formed in bas-relief in mud over the
openings of mud homes. Sometimes the house and cross are
brick. The Copts, who are fond of reading the family Bible
at home, are aware of Exodus 12:13 and the significance of
a sign in order to escape the wrath of the Lord: "And the
blood shall be to you for a token upon the houses where ye

are: and when I see the blood, I will pass over you, and the
plague shall not be upon you to destroy you, when I smite
the land of Egypt."

The cross is highly functional for a minority living in an
inhospitable environment. It labels the friendly house for
the traveler and if a man is taken ill away from home, his
tattoo readily identifies him as a Christian. His children can't
be kidnapped and claimed as Moslems if the cross is upon
them. And if he dies where he is not known, his cross tattoo
will guarantee a Christian burial. The tattoo is also used by
beggars to solicit Christian alms and by clerks in Egyptian
bazaars to swear by (to convince the c stomer that the price
is right). It makes it difficult for a girl to become a prostitute
and disgrace her church and community as well as family
and it is most awkward to have on your wrist if you want
to turn Moslem. In rural Egypt, as a missionary nun observed
Copts brand their animals to identify them and "mark their
children as their own."

After centuries of neglect under an indifferent and ignorant clergy, the cross stands in the midst of an assortment of
superstitions and primitive practices such as the cure for
dog bite administered by a Coptic priest. It is used by Moslems as well as Copts. Seven children, seven dates, seven
pieces of bread and a jug of water are part of a ceremony
in which the Coptic priest recites prayers and then makes
the victim eat one date, one piece of bread and drink one
swallow of water. The victim continues this daily dosage
until cured.

The superstitions include magical formulas that make
barren women fruitful, increase wages and the crop, and
combat the evil eye, all common Egyptian preoccupations
One schoolboy was employed by his grandfather during his
vacations, reading formulas from the "Book of the Seven
Angels." (Seven is a favorite Coptic number.) Long lines of
women paid a few piasters each in order to have the for-

mulas read over them. If the evil spirit appears after a man's death, the Coptic priest is summoned and he goes to the place of appearance armed with a palm branch and a jug of water. He makes the evil spirit enter the jug and then buries it or throws it away in the desert.

Such practices were observed in recent years by scholars at the Coptic Institute—a Catholic organization distinct from the newer Higher Institute of Coptic Studies—and they reflect the state of the church, particularly in rural Egypt. Understandably, the Catholic missionaries have accommodated themselves to the condition of Egyptian Christianity. A Franciscan priest in close contact with the Vatican and its missionary policy summed up the approach: "Catholic missionaries in Egypt realize they must work for a strong Coptic Church. The Vatican wants its missionaries to strengthen the Coptic Church. Better a good Copt than a bad Catholic. We have no right to sow doubt where the people are sure of their religion, but Catholic missionaries do make converts where the people are left unclaimed, like property that has been unclaimed."

Although the Coptic and Catholic churches normally cooperate in Egypt, there is little hope of any Coptic rapprochement with Rome. Historically, approaches have been made by the Vatican in the 13th, 15th and 17th centuries; the latter might have succeeded if it weren't for the behavior and attitude of the European Catholics living in Cairo. In the 18th century when the Coptic bishop in Jerusalem turned Catholic, he was placed in charge of the Catholic Copts in Egypt, but feelings were so strong against him that he could never set foot in Egypt. The first Catholic Coptic Patriarch was appointed in 1895 and resigned in 1908, leaving the Catholic chair vacant until 1947. It is obvious that the Copts regard union with Rome as a threat to their identity and while some join the Catholic Coptic Church, such conversions have limited impact.

The Protestant missionaries, who arrived originally to convert the Moslems, soon switched from this hopeless cause to the neglected Christians. The Presbyterians reported in 1953 after their first hundred years that they had about 100 Moslem converts and about 100,000 Copts. Those Copts who have become active in the Protestant churches are noticeably Westernized and tend to develop the same style as their Western teachers.

To a large extent, all the missionaries in Egypt have succeeded by claiming unclaimed property and in the process they have helped to revitalize the Coptic Church. Evidence of their influence turns up in different ways. Coptic priests introduced sermons at Mass when Protestant sermons began to attract Copts. In Alexandria, when the Franciscans made headway after World War II, the church finally paid attention to the Copts living in the city's slums and several new churches were opened. The prewar total of five churches in Alexandria has tripled or quadrupled since the war, depending on which estimate is used. A missionary in an Upper Egyptian town reported that his attendance at Coptic services as a gesture of good will brought out larger church attendance by the Copts themselves. The missionaries, reminders of neglect and examples of energetic churchmanship, have stimulated the Coptic Church to keep its members within the flock.

In the process, the Protestant and Catholic clergymen have witnessed a revival within the Coptic Church and they are impressed by its vigor. Though the revival was certainly developing before the present Patriarch was seated, his ineffectual predecessor was an albatross the church never could fully shake as long as he lived. The heart of the revival is the youth movement manifested by the flourishing Sunday School program and by the new blood among clergy and monks. True to their commitment to the church, the laity have made both developments possible.

The ambitious Sunday School program reportedly has one million students between the ages of 5 and 16, 4,000 branches and more than 5,000 volunteer teachers. Begun in 1908 and revised in 1930, the Sunday School movement gained momentum in the early 1940's with a nationwide promotion campaign that far surpassed the previous quota of one church, one Sunday School. Though the statistics are undoubtedly exaggerated, the church has succeeded in organizing and maintaining a large-scale operation and it provides the church with a network of branches and loyal workers. While strengthening the Copts as a group, the Sunday School program should be immune to political supression by a Moslem-dominated regime. The only formal lessons are religious, though each pupil represents an explicit commitment by his parents to the Coptic identity. At an impressionable age the child learns where he belongs as he receives the emotional message of Christ and the Cross.

In many churches, the Sunday School movement has reached the next stage of youth fellowship groups. For instance, in the Giza Church, a young men's group meets on Thursday afternoons and a young women's group on Wednesday afternoons while Sunday School classes are held on Sundays and Fridays. (Government schools are closed on Fridays in observance of the Moslem holy day.)

In 1958 a lay religious movement was begun with headquarters in Helwan, near Cairo, in a converted palace once used by an Egyptian princess. Under the guidance of Abuna Matta al-Maskin, the influential monk from the Monastery of St. Samuel, a small group of young men, including a doctor and government schoolteachers, have pledged their lives to the church. They intend to remain celibate and aim eventually to serve the church full-time as laymen. At present, they are engaged in a modified communal life built around their working days and have also been publishing religious books. One of the group defined the need they hope to meet:

"A great number of our clergy are not doing their work
They just perform the liturgy, but they do not work with
the people."

The internal situation of the church has been summed
up before. In *Twentieth Century Impressions of Egypt*—
published in 1909—an article on the Copts reported: "But
the inexorable law of progress is now beginning to affect
even this seclusive community. Among the younger generation of Copts, many of whom have been educated according
to Western notions and have become imbued with Western
ideas, has arisen a feeling of dissatisfaction with the condition of stagnation and obsoleteness, begotten of many cen
turies of subjection to Mohammedan rule, to which then
Church has been reduced."

Two generations later, similar dissatisfaction appeared
in Giza, home of the Pyramids and the University of Cairo
(then Fuad University). University students formed an advanced "Sunday School" in the mid-1930's that met Thursday evenings under the direction of professors from the old
Coptic Theological College. Out of this Giza Movement
which had as many as 50 university students at one time
came highly-committed laymen and some of the outstanding
priests and monks in the church today.

"We were very angry with the way hings were in the
church," a leader of the group recalled. "We wanted to
study the old church in order to revive the modern church
The priests weren't preaching, they didn't visit the people,
they didn't keep any records. We wanted to revive the function of deacon and to have him teach Sunday School, preach
assist priests, help the poor." (There are three main orders
of clergy: bishop, priest and deacon, plus four su divisions
reader, sub-deacon, arch-deacon and arch-priest.)

Ten years later, about 10 priests and more than 15 monks
were recruited from the Giza Movement, small in number
but enough to set an example before an apathetic clergy and

a dissatisfied laity. Characteristically, the pull of the monastery was stronger than that of the parish church and the transfusions came from the community. These new priests and monks were university graduates, many of them pharmacists and engineers, who turned their backs on successful careers. They were not community leftovers, and they have since been joined by others of equal caliber.

To maintain a flow of competent clergy, the Coptic Seminary is training about 150 full-time students divided into two levels, depending on whether or not they graduated from secondary school. About 30 university graduates also attend the seminary's night classes while they work days. According to responsible estimates, the seminary training is sound, surpassing the indifferent standards of its predecessor institution. Some graduates will become priests immediately, while others will become priests in 15 or 20 years in line with the tendency toward late vocations (which seem to provide the most effective Coptic priests). Other graduates become preachers or teachers in religious schools.

Since the Copts are a group constantly engaged in conversation about themselves, a few examples go a long way. One priest frequently cited is Abuna Boulos Boulos of Damanhur, the Patriarch's home town. (Also site of a historical footnote: On July 10, 1798, near the town, Napoleon became isolated from his main army during his invasion of Egypt and narrowly escaped capture by the Mamelukes). Abuna Boulos, who was mainly responsible for the Giza "Sunday School," graduated from the university in 1940 and worked for ten years as an irrigation engineer for the government and as a deacon for the church. In 1950, he went on a Thursday, his day off, to the local bishop, who ordained him, and he became the new priest at Damanhur. His government department, taken by surprise, proceeded to pay him two weeks' accrued vacation after he had become a priest.

The incongruity of his brief distinction as a Coptic priest
in the pay of the Egyptian government is not lost on Abuna
Boulos. He is a hearty, three-quarter-sized version of Burl
Ives. Though he was sick in bed the day we visited him, his
black beard bounced on top of a white coverlet as he talked
good-naturedly about himself, his family and his people. He
introduced the people in the room: "This is my doctor. He
is a Copt. Here is my oldest son. He is a Copt. My wife is
a Copt, and even I am a Copt." He introduced a priest from
a neighboring town. "You see how our work succeeds. He
was a deacon here in my church and an engineer like myself.
Four months ago he became a priest." At one point, two
dozen young ladies who teach Sunday School trooped through
the room in single file, paying their respects briefly and kiss-
ing his hand. As several other parishioners streamed into the
small bedroom, it was obvious that they were not coming
merely to honor a priestly symbol. He was their shepherd.

In Damanhur, the Copts needed a shepherd as much as
anywhere in Egypt. In this drab Delta town, whose main
street reaches the main highway after cutting through what
looks like a frontier settlement from the American Wild
West, the odds are long. About 96 percent of the population
of 120,000 is Moslem, their mentality backward, their resources limited and their attitude ranging from hostility to
indifference. Before Abuna Boulos' arrival, there was only
one Coptic church, dating back to 1848, which typified the
stagnant churches of Egypt.

Abuna Boulos has in effect defined the role facing the new
breed of Coptic priests. They must commit themselves to
the total identity of the Copts and their total situation, offering advice and leadership for the minority as well as religious
outlets. Abuna Boulos, who visits each Coptic family three
times a year, points out that "we cannot sit at home, but
must go out and do something with personal contact." His
church has become a social as well as a religious center and

he has become the contact between the Copts and local government officials.

His style has caught the attention of young priests in the string of Coptic churches from Alexandria to Cairo, for this priest with his jolly holiness helped to break the ancient mold in the Egyptian church. He is neither self-seeking nor indifferent but constantly concerned about his flock—and he is competent. When last seen, he was saying for the fifth or sixth time that he wanted a movie camera in order to make religious films in the little theater attached to his church. He talked with childish delight at the prospect of being a movie producer in that one-horse Delta town. But he was serious about it; he knows his Copts well.

The future of the Coptic Church in Egypt will undoubtedly depend more on such practical piety than on the melodramatic posture of the monk. From a supernatural viewpoint as stated by a leading Western clergyman in Cairo, "If God wants the Coptic Church to continue, he will inspire the needed leadership and clergy." Dr. Attulah, head of the Coptic Seminary, estimates the need as 4,000 priests, four to five times the current total.

The measure of the breakthrough symbolized by Abuna Boulos is the Coptic priest who was asked to say something in Coptic by a visiting Western lady trying to be polite. He replied with the Greek phrase "Kyrie eleison." Or the priest in an Upper Egyptian church who could be found only with difficulty on a visit to his locked church and then he didn't have a key to open it. When the caretaker was found, the history of his church had to be explained by parishioners. Or the three priests and their families who act as caretakers of the ancient White Monastery, no longer used by monks but honored as a shrine. There, about 300 miles south of Cairo, the priests' children play and go to school and their wives keep house. The idle ones are the priests who, as one of the women said, receive visitors who bring gifts, supervise the lands belonging to the monastery, and pray. "That's all they do," she added. Between Abuna Boulos and the idle bearded priests in soiled black frocks at the White Monastery lies the gap between the new and the old in the Coptic clergy, reasons for past decline and future hope.

CHAPTER XIV

The Community of Copts

In the back of the Coptic Guide of 1950, a simple pullout
map depicts the fertile area of the Nile Valley in a literal
green, making Egypt's 4 percent of habitable land look
like a lotus flower with its petals flattened at the Mediterranean shore and its thin stem reaching south to the Sudan.
Spread throughout flower and stem are the names of towns
and cities that sound like exotic terms in a botany lesson.
In each the Copts had effective units of self-government
called Community Councils (Maglis Milli). In addition to
Cairo and Alexandria, local Councils functioned in Damanhur, Tanta, Mansoura, Zagazig, Dayrut, Shibin al-Kum,
Giza, Fayoum, Beni Suef, Minia, Maghagha, Manfalut, Assyut, Abutig, Guergueh, Sohag, al-Balyana, Qena and Isna.
Five elected representatives sat on each Council, with the
exception of Alexandria where there were seven. In Cairo,
the general Council of 23 elected members represented the
entire community of Copts.

This network of Councils formed the outline of an inner
flower and stem on the Coptic map of Egypt, theoretically
the framework for a Coptic nation within the Egyptian nation. While foreign affairs, defense, irrigation, and control of

147

the Nile flood were in government hands, such domestic matters as personal rights, religious affairs, education and social welfare could be handled by the Copts themselves. Thus, the Community Councils, established in 1873, theoretically offered the opportunity for an important measure of Coptic self-rule, its roots in Islamic tradition and in the bureaucratic structure of the Ottoman Empire.

The Islamic basis for the Coptic Community Council is the traditional division of the populace into self-contained religious communities. This was formalized by the Ottoman Turks into a system of horizontal administrative units called millets. Organized under the direction of the highest ecclesiastical dignitary, the millet controlled civil as well as religious matters for the members of the church. It even had the power to levy taxes on behalf of the government.

In the late nineteenth century during one of their attempts at church reformation, leading Copts mixed church precedent with Islamic tradition and Ottoman policy in order to end the clerical monopoly of power. The millet had made the Patriarch dominant; the Community Council was devised to establish a partnership with the laity. The necessary precedent was found in a thirteenth century collection of the Canons of the Church of Egypt, which stated: "In all important matters the Patriarch must consult learned and pious men, both priests and laymen, singly and collectively." The result was the 1873 plan for a general Community Council and local Councils of laymen authorized to supervise financial and personal affairs. Not only were the bishops persuaded to accept the plan, but a government decree was also obtained to give added legitimacy to the Council. The celebrated Butros Pasha Ghali engineered issuance of the decree by the Khedive ruling at the time.

Four general functions were assigned to the Community Council: Administrative—assist the clergy in running the church. Educational—provide religious and general educa-

tion for Copts. Financial—plan the church budget. Judicial
—operate the religious court for personal status cases. On
the local level, the number of cases involving such matters
as divorce, custody of children and wills ranged annually
from 120 in Assyut and 60 in Qena to 500 in Cairo (where
there was a local as well as general Council). Local decisions
on schools, church property and divorce were subject to approval by the general Council. Both voters and Council candidates still must meet requirements based on education and
income, which, appropriately, are the main Coptic status
symbols.

In theory, the Copts had a lay-clerical partnership designed for vigorous Coptic coexistence with Moslems. Instead, the hierarchy and laity engaged in a frustrating in-
ternecine contest that began with the attempted reformation
of 1873 and continued through the reign of the kidnapped
Patriarch of the 1950's. This is not surprising. Before the
partnership could succeed, both sides would have to sur-
render narrow interests in favor of a commitment to the
community as a whole. This is a lesson in cooperation that
still has not been learned throughout the Middle East. The
hierarchy would have to loosen their grip on personal prerogatives and end the corruption of pomp and circumstance.
The laity would have to abandon their characteristic tendency to feud, intrigue and maneuver, and acquire a spirit of
compromise. There was neither precedent nor inclination
for such changes.

Basically, it was a church-state struggle within the confines
of the Coptic minority. The Copts had to settle which was
paramount: church or community. Are Copts primarily
members of an ancient Christian church or members of a
persistently identifiable community of Egyptians? The answer seems obvious to the outsider. The community is more
inclusive than the church, many Copts are indifferent to the
church but highly committed to their community, the

church limped into the twentieth century while the community was thriving. But the hierarchy, which has vested interests, formal authority and, in many cases, strong religious
motivation, could not accept a secondary place for the
church.

The struggle between the general Council and its
hierarchical counterpart, the Holy Synod of bishops, in alliance with the monks, was expressed in a legalism: whether
the Council's power to supervise the financial affairs of the
church extended to actual administration. The prize was
control of the waqfs, a total of 9,000 valuable acres left as
religious endowments to the church and to monasteries. The
latter held about two-thirds of these acres which were worth,
in all, eighteen million dollars if the standard selling price
of two thousand dollars an acre were applied.

The issue of controlling the waqfs obsessed the Coptic
community in the ensuing decades with both the tactics
and the incidents reappearing with frustrating regularity:
promises made and broken by Patriarchs, banishments of
Patriarchs, appeals to the courts and even to the Moslem
regime to solve what the Copts could not or would not solve
themselves. Both Kirillus V, who was Patriarch when the
Council was established, and Yusab II, predecessor of the
present Patriarch, had promised to cooperate with the laity
prior to their election, and both reneged. Yusab's downfall
began when he was confronted with the agreement he signed
as Bishop of Guergeh, promising to support control of the
waqfs by the Community Council. He reportedly replied:
"The Bishop of Guergeh signed it, not the Patriarch." Eventually both Patriarchs were banished, though Kirillus did
return in temporary triumph.

Out of this habitual struggle came the consistent evasion
of community problems as candidates for the Council made
their stand on the issues of waqf control and patriarchal
election procedures. These teapot controversies became ends

in themselves, unrelated to the goals of reform, and the Community Council never faced the need to mobilize community resources and achieve community-wide cooperation. Failing to solve internal problems, the Council never confronted the external issue of coexistence with the Moslem majority. No machinery of complaint was established and the Council never represented the community to the government in power. Cooperating in the blindness of the hierarchy, leading laymen closed their eyes to the decline of community and church and Copts were left to grumble about internal weakness and external discrimination—privately and among themselves.

Finally, Nasser ended the waqf controversy in the summer of 1960 with Republican Decree No. 264 which limited each waqf holding to about 200 acres of cultivable and 200 of barren land. The rest were nationalized and the Agrarian Reform Authority was authorized to take over the excess holdings of any waqf and pay cash to the church in exchange. The Patriarch, Kirillus VI, dutifully hailed the government decree, not without good reason. "It will lead to the proper organization of the Coptic waqfs which previously always caused dissension among the Coptic people," the Patriarch said. "It will also enable the value of the exchanged land to be used in industrial and reconstruction projects being carried out by the Revolution." The Coptic weekly, "Watani," hailed the removal of "the stone on which all the effort of the good people of the Coptic Church was wasted for almost an entire century."

Power over the waqfs was placed in the hands of a new body, the Coptic Orthodox Waqfs Organization. Its members were named by the Patriarch from the two divergent bodies, the Holy Synod and the Community Council, with effective control in the hands of the church. This was the coup de grace for the Council. It had already lost its judicial powers with the abolition of religious courts in 1955; now its financial powers were drastically reduced.

Leading Copts rushed to write its epitaph, as if the Council were the cause of the community's tensions rather than the victim. A prominent Coptic leader called the Council "just a souvenir" and Antun Sidhum, publisher of "Watani," said, "We want the government to cancel the Community Council. It has done nothing during the troubles of recent years. During all its existence the Council has only caused trouble; it has spent the past eighty years quarreling with the Patriarch. We want to abolish it. It has lost its function."

An opposite view, which was still being expressed a year after Nasser nationalized the waqfs, stressed the limitations of the church's role. "Watani" quoted the leading member of the Alexandria Community Council, Judge Farid Pharaony:

"The Community Council is a necessity. Through it, the people can handle financial matters and direct their own affairs. The only thing the priest can handle is the spiritual. We members of the Community Council don't have any vested interest in the management of community affairs since we are not getting any salaries."

Before the nationalization of waqfs, the Council in Cairo had an income of 60,000 Egyptian pounds from land and 30,000 pounds from buildings that comprised waqf properties unqualifiedly under its control. Though small in comparison with the monastery waqfs, the Council waqfs financed the following allocations in 1959: 21,000 pounds for churches and priests in Cairo, 16,000 for the Coptic Seminary, 13,000 for employees, 10,000 for running the patriarchal establishment, and 5,000 for the Coptic Institute.

The prerogatives left to the Council are illustrated by the actions of the new general Council elected in the summer of 1961. That fall, at a meeting with 35 items on the agenda, it approved designs for three apartment house on patriarchal land, accepted social security benefits for patriarchal employees and allocated funds for building a clerical college and renovating a monastery.

Fundamentally, the Council's troubles exposed the failure of community leadership. Leading Copts have refused to accept the responsibilities of their opportunity for internal democracy and have shunned militancy, either because their businesses would suffer or their relatives might lose government positions or because they were reluctant to lead when they had no confidence others would follow. Accordingly, the Council members have submitted to the role of the cooperative public Copt. In the midst of general unrest in the community and of multiplying evidence of discrimination, the new Council held its first meeting on October 1, 1961, soon after Syria made its abrupt exit from the United Arab Republic. Its first official act was to send a telegram of "encouragement" to Nasser in his time of trouble.

Though the Community Council has been reduced to a loyal whimper and Coptic leadership to empty formalities, there is renewed vigor in the community nonetheless. The Copts, like stubborn farmers clinging to inhospitable soil, are planting new seeds and caring for the surviving crops, thereby asserting determination to maintain and cultivate their identity. The evidence is present in the campaign to resurrect the moribund Coptic language, to glorify and reconstitute Coptic culture, in educational activity and in their continuing social welfare activities. This evidence is not overwhelming, but it does fit into the picture of Coptic renaissance.

The Coptic language is a case in point. Its revival is impractical, as pointed out by a scholarly Jesuit in a short treatise in 1953 on Coptic religious customs, yet it is psychologically important, as demonstrated by children studying the Coptic language in an outdoor class in Alexandria. The Jesuit noted that it is no longer a national language; it is a "venerable monument and deserves the same care and respect as ancient temples." But in the composition books of the little girls in the Alexandria class, the Coptic language exercises keep repeating, in effect: "I am a Copt, I am a Copt . . ." The class—an improvised scene, an imitation outdoor catacomb set up without danger behind a wall of billboard signs —was observed in the dirt yard of a gymnasium once used by the Armenians and now converted into a Coptic church. Inside the church, the liturgy was being celebrated on a Saturday in August; outside two men and a young woman supervised a class of 24 schoolgirls. After the service, the black-robed, bearded priests good-naturedly inspected the work of the students, girls in bright cotton dresses attending the church's summer school three days a week and learning who they are.

In 1961, the education committee of the Community Council ordered the inclusion of Coptic language classes in all Sunday Schools. A program of study was drawn up, teachers were recruited and annual prizes announced for the best students. A program of summer classes for adults was also announced, though there already were an estimated 1,000 adults studying the Coptic language. Here and there, signs of language revival turn up. A new book on teaching the Coptic language was presented to the Patriarch and he was welcomed on a visit to Helwan with a speech in Coptic. Some 20 families in Cairo are using it as a household language, including the family of the Coptic Museum director. He summarized the desire for identification when he said: "We want to speak the language of our ancestors."

The interest in the Coptic language belongs to a general cultural revival noted in the early 1940's by the leading U. S. authority on the Copts, the late Professor William H. Worrell, who wrote: "In non-clerical circles, individuals among the younger generation of Copts with more or less of a European training are creating a respect for the Coptic past and a strictly scientific treatment of its remains." Under the direction of an able scholar, Dr. Bahour Labib Akladios, and with the support of government funds, the Coptic Museum in Old Cairo houses an extensive collection of Coptic antiquities, manuscripts, intricate wood paneling, paintings, sculpture and, in particular, the varied religious objects of early churches and monasteries. The Museum abounds in a double documentation: artifacts of early Christianity and evidence of the Coptic bridge between Pharaonic and Islamic art. For historical reminders, there are several representations of St. George, the celebrated dragon killer who is still a visible favorite in Coptic churches and households, and massive iron-re-enforced doors once used to seal off the Coptic sections at night from Moslem marauders.

Professor Worrell called the Museum, which dates back to 1908, the "material center of interest in Coptic art and archeology and a guarantee of the continuance and growth of that interest." But the newly-established (1954) Higher Institute of Coptic Studies now surpasses it in importance to the community. Under the direction of a renowned archeologist, Dr. Sami Gabra, the Institute is approaching its stated goal of raising "the standard of academic studies in the fields of Coptic culture." An ambitious postgraduate enterprise, it is becoming an intellectual rallying point for both faculty and students who want to bring the Coptic heritage up to date. The Institute's ten sections embrace art and archeology, the laws and theology of the church, area studies of Africa and Ethiopia, social studies and microfilming of Coptic antiquities in monasteries and churches. Each student is required to study both the Coptic language and church history.

The Institute's faculty even convinced the present Patriarch that the January 7 date of the Coptic Christmas had no historic validity and should be changed to coincide with the Western date of December 25. The dramatic change, which would have included Easter as well, had the added tactical merit of drawing Egypt's Christians closer together. But the arguments from history were outweighed by a clique of reactionary bishops supported by businessmen with a vested interest in the January 7 date. The Patriarch backed down. Disappointed, a leading member of the Institute applied a Coptic euphemism to the Patriarch's vacillation; he could have had his way but he is a "man of peace."

The Institute has suffered from the Coptic proclivity for feuding. One of its chief architects claimed this has "practically immobilized" the Institute, with battle lines drawn "not on intellectual terms but on the basis of personal animosities." (Echoes of the Community Council.)

Overall, the Institute still represents a giant step forward. Under its aegis, social studies are attempted, historical and cultural research pursued and modernizing ideas ventilated. In one case, an art professor designed a streamlined Coptic church merging modern design and the tradition of the early Christian Era in Nubia. The proposed church looks like an elongated modern ship whose bell tower is separate and whose entrance is a ramp instead of stairs. It is still there on the drawing board, but a seed of change was planted.

At the Institute, located near Cairo's Ramses Street about a hundred yards behind a gasoline station, a religious-cultural-intellectual center of Coptic life is in the making. Plans include new facilities for the clerical college, the Institute and St. Mark's College as well as a modern school for the blind. Presumably, these plans will be supported by the government's promised cash payments for nationalized waqf lands.

Thus far, the Copts have had little success in establishing a vigorous press of their own. At the moment they have one decrepit daily newspaper and one well-edited and docile weekly, "Watani." An assortment of miscellaneous magazines emanate from different organizations and churches, but their editorial whisper is hardly heard outside their small following of duty-bound readers. The Coptic daily, "Misr," was once the dominant voice in the affairs of the church and its editor a channel for patriarchal appointments and royal favors. The last time anyone listened to its voice was in the clamor against the previous Patriarch. Under the present Patriarch, the paper is reduced to 3,000 diehard readers, a ramshackle office, and a "safe" editor who works mornings for the official government news agency. "Misr" is dying unlamented. The Patriarch was asked to take over the paper, but he refused.

"Watani," which began publication November 20, 1958, is financed by wealthy Copts who wanted a reputable community voice. It has reached a circulation of about 40,000 by offering a Sunday morning mixture of world, national, Hollywood, and parochial Coptic news and features. Though its publisher talks unconvincingly of his weekly as a rallying point for Copts, "Watani" is no more than can be expected in a country without a free press and with newspapers that remain in business at the pleasure of the regime. The government's permission to launch "Watani" is regarded as a small Nasser favor for which there is little gratitude.

The main outlet for community zeal has been the Coptic organizations which have proliferated since the turn of the century. Most numerous in Cairo, these exclusively Coptic organizations teach the young, shelter orphans, care for the sick, the poor and the handicapped, help pay marriage expenses, provide social and recreational outlets, and bury the dead. In effect, they maintain a closed circle of Coptic activities, enabling the individual to fulfill his personal needs within the community. It is a doubly re-enforced circle, reenforced from within by the Copts and from without by Moslem rejection.

The sustained interest in community needs is evident in

a directory of Cairo private social agencies registered with the Ministry of Social Affairs in 1955. A total of 104 Coptic organizations are listed, dating back to the late nineteenth century. Since the directory covered only slightly more than half of the 1,167 registered agencies, the current Coptic estimate of 250 organizations in Cairo is plausible, though many are only paper organizations.

The stated purposes listed by the Coptic organizations center on three dominant themes: education, assistance for the weak and needy, and support of religious commitments. The laity, in maintaining these organizations, is not only making the implicit statement that the church is unwilling or unable to meet community needs. More than that, the laity has included the care and feeding of the Coptic religion in its responsibilities, reaffirming the church's secondary position.

Beginning with the Society for the Welfare of Coptic Children in the village of Zeitoun (founded late in 1961), a random list of typical Coptic organizations can move backwards over the decades, showing how each new organization founded by laymen phrases its statement of intention to look after the community's members:

Samaret al-Mahaba Coptic Association—Founded in 1951 "to establish a handicraft workshop for girls and a dispensary; extend financial aid to the needy; spread the principles of Christianity."

Coptic Orthodox Reawakening Youth Association—Founded in 1945 "to establish Sunday Schools, a dispensary and an orphanage; organize groups of sextons; teach the Bible and the Coptic language; extend financial assistance and provide burial facilities to underprivileged families."

Al-Nahda Coptic Orthodox Youth Association—Founded in 1936 "to preach, counsel, and train sexton groups; establish Sunday Schools, a hospital, a social club and an orphanage; extend aid to the underprivileged."

Al-Malak al-Quebli Benevolent Association at Old Cairo
—Founded in 1927 "to sponsor a church; preach and counsel; establish schools, orphanages and dispensaries in Old Cairo; extend financial assistance, including aid for marriage expenses and burial facilities to the underprivileged."

Coptic Benevolent Institute—Founded in 1917 "to sponsor the education of Coptic Orthodox underprivileged children and orphans."

Al-Mahaba Coptic Orthodox Benevolent Association—Founded in 1902 "to provide educational facilities to underprivileged Coptic Orthodox girls."

In 1890, al-Tewfik Society was formed as an outgrowth of the same dissatisfaction and demand for church reform that led to establishment of the Community Council. The society issued pamphlets in order to arouse public opinion to the need for reform, though, as Mrs. Butcher notes with chagrin, "the original desire for reform was obscured for the time in the struggle for the upper hand."

In 1960, I watched the al-Tewfik Coptic Benevolent Association usher in the Coptic new year in the courtyard of a multiple enterprise in community service, encompassing two primary and two intermediate schools, a technical school, an out-patient clinic, a hospital and an undertaker's shop. The inescapable lesson of the al-Tewfik Association, which has thrived since its founding, and the Community Council, which has floundered, is that the Copts are ready to help each other, but not to unite, and no one is ready or able to lead them as a community.

CHAPTER XV

The Home of the Copts

The attachment of Copts to their Egyptian homeland is dramatized in the small-scale diaspora of the young, the educated and the qualified who have begun to leave Egypt. They leave with reluctance, talking not of greener pastures elsewhere but of closed doors at home. Feeling deprived of the traditional Coptic right to market their skills at a reasonably high price, they turn to the last resort of departure and dispersion.

Yet the trappings of the Coptic identity are not suited to long journeys. Its symbols and ceremonies need the church and clergy which are left behind, while departure breaks the closed circle of community life. Copts, already Westernized, become invisible in a Western country. In another Middle East country, they blend into the mosaic of Arab Christian minorities. If the Copt continues to attend church abroad, he will go to a Greek Orthodox church or an Eastern Catholic church. Sometimes, he chooses a Protestant church. It's a matter of personal predilection. The Copt travels lightly, bringing mainly his skills and flexibility in the marketplace. What was useful to the Ottoman Empire, the British occupation and the Farouk regime is still marketable in Beirut, London and Chicago.

Time and distance will eventually erase nostalgia for Egypt, but one link is bound to survive during the lifetime of the dispersed Copt—his family commitment. This locates the answer to the centuries of Coptic survival, for the family unit is the solid, unyielding foundation on which the unsteady structures of church and community have stood. In the final analysis, the minority has survived because each family in each Coptic home has sustained the group's identity and has dug its roots into the Nile Valley. In this dependence on the family, the Coptic minority does not differ from other durable minorities, whether the Jews with their miracle of survival over the centuries, the long-suffering Armenians, or the ethnic groups remaining intact inside the so-called American melting pot.

A brilliant Coptic engineer now becoming a successful organization man in New York City still writes his mother daily, and when he mentions his lingering uncertainty about deserting Egypt, he says with more meaning than he intends: "After all, Egypt is my mother." Enclosed within the home in which he was reared was the response to the challenge of survival. Each generation of each family handed identity to the next, a relay race pursued over the centuries and summed up in the ultimate simplicity of an individual Copt's statement on his identity: "I was born a Copt. That's why I'm a Copt."

In the beginning of life, as one Coptic father stated, "Children are baptized on the faith of their fathers and mothers who are held responsible before God for bringing up children in the Coptic faith." Godparents, normally chosen from the family, re-enforce the commitment. The child is named after a grandparent, a favorite saint or a favorite relative, depending on the desire of the parents, though some families decide by burning three candles each representing a different name. The candle that burns longest—symbolizing a long life—names the child.

With his parents, brothers and sisters as the nucleus, each Coptic child becomes increasingly entangled in relationships on both sides of the family that reach beyond uncles and aunts to distant cousins. By the time he grows up, he can run across a marriage announcement in the newspaper and trace the girl's relationship to him on his mother's side by the marriage of a great-aunt to a lawyer from Assyut. In lines that are clear and unmistakable, the individual Copt knows the details of his extended family relationships, each demanding varying degrees of loyalty and responsibility.

While the Coptic family resembles the traditional European family in many ways, it differs sharply from the Moslem family which is constantly imperiled by divorces that complicate the child's position. The Moslems have a saying that reflects (and exaggerates) the insecurity of a wife: "When a woman prepares a meal for her husband, she is not sure she will be his wife long enough to share it." Many Moslem children grow up with substitute parents who are often uncles and aunts, sometimes servants. Though the Moslem woman is moving out of her traditional position of inferiority, Coptic women have always been more emancipated and the mother has been in a special position. The Coptic husband, unlike the Moslem, is likely to joke about being henpecked. The Coptic father, particularly in middle class families, centers his life around the home, which is less disturbed by the centrifugal pull of divorce, the coffee house and a male vanity culture that tends to keep the Moslem father in exclusively male company.

The Coptic child receives very early the message from his father that he must do well in school for the sake of his parents, his family and, also, for himself. He learns to honor the ritual of family gatherings on Sunday as he is thrown into close contact with his cousins of the same age. Holy days, weddings, birthdays and anniversaries become occasions for mandatory family gatherings. There is little opportunity to go beyond the family circle and less beyond the circle of Copts. The dramatic highlights of the child's life become his first Communion and his Confirmation.

Except to establish a family of their own or attend a university, Coptic sons and daughters ordinarily never leave home. Even when a son returns from Oxford, the Sorbonne or N.Y.U. and begins a successful professional career, he remains with his parents until he marries. Bachelor apartments are practically unheard of. Until about thirty years ago, the son brought his wife into his father's household, though the modern fashion is to set up separate households while still honoring all family obligations. Eventually, the son takes his aged parents into his household, completing the life cycle of intimate relationship between child and parent. At death, the parents are interred in the family's special burial grounds, a symbolic area where the solidarity of the family is reaffirmed and homage paid regularly to the dead.

In love and marriage, cousins or children of known and respected families are preferred. Until recent years, first-cousin marriages were common, thereby keeping a tight rein on property and protecting the family from outsiders. Reluctantly, Coptic families have accepted foreigners married by sons away at school, though the resistance to such marriages is supported by the fact that many of the dispersed Copts have married non-Copts.

Since parental approval is still regarded as mandatory, prospective wives and husbands are screened by the family, though in many cases this is unnecessary because cousins or close family friends are involved. Coptic mothers often act as go-betweens in matching couples. If the prospective mate is from the father's side of the family, his opinion is paramount, vice versa if the mate is from the mother's side, though generally speaking mother negotiates and father decides. In conservative families, boy and girl meet and court in the presence of the family. Dating alone is still not common. Even when the family is not around, couples go out in groups. Engagements occur after both families agree, and once this is settled, the engagements are not prolonged beyond six to twelve months. Parents want to reduce the risk of complications in a long engagement, for the match does not pretend to be merely a matter between two individuals. It involves both families.

The betrothal, formalized by a priest with the standard supporting cast of chanters with incense and cymbals, takes place in the home before family and friends and is regarded as "half a wedding." Technically, the betrothal is part of the actual wedding ceremony and needs church approval to be dissolved. The marriage ceremony omits the betrothal formula if it already has been pronounced and proceeds to anoint, crown and join in wedlock. Normally, wedding ceremonies are performed in church, though in rural areas they often take place in the home. The couple are supposed to partake of two other sacraments as well as matrimony: confession and Communion.

At one summer wedding witnessed in the fashionable Cairo suburb of Heliopolis, the ceremony inside the church was counterpointed outdoors by a composite view of middle class family life. In the social and recreation area adjoining the church, children played games and pleaded for soda pop, teenagers played basketball, nubile young ladies sat under watchful eyes at tables where parents chatted with friends. In the same Heliopolis, renowned in the ancient world for its temple to the Sun god Ra, Coptic fathers in short-sleeved nylon shirts and mothers in Pharaonic print dresses testified to the saga of Coptic continuity, though the scene was as exotic as a Little League father-and-son outing.

At the church, the congregation, arriving desultorily and late, took their places, looking about, nodding to friends, then became vaguely attentive to the proceedings. (Sometimes it seems that the Coptic church clashes its cymbals and breaks into outbursts of chanting in order to catch the attention of its congregation.) At the altar, the giggling bride turned repeatedly to whisper to her bridesmaids and to her flower girls; the groom, wearing white ceremonial vestments over his formal suit of clothes, patiently endured the chanting, the cymbals, the incense. At one point, pieces of candy wrapped in cellophane were distributed; at another point during the ceremony, gigantic wreaths of red, pink and white flowers were brought in. The clothes worn by the congregation ranged from the traditional all-black ensembles of older ladies accompanied by husbands in white suits to stout ladies in brocade dresses, servant girls in faded cottons and little girls dressed in ruffles. According to church teaching, the ceremony conferred on the couple the grace to live together in mutual love and purity. Adultery, that eternal threat to the family, is regarded as the most reprehensible sin by the Copts. (If a son kills his father, it is said that the victim is not his father, thereby linking the murder to adultery.)

At marriage, the bride and groom transfer the gold bands which they exchanged at their betrothal from the right to the left hand. The husband strains his resources to give his bride a diamond ring; she symbolizes their new intimacy with a gift of bedroom slippers, pajamas and a dressing gown. The bride's family, which pays for her trousseau, furnishes the bedroom in their new home, often the living and dining rooms as well. Since the bride retains any inherited wealth for her own use and great stress is placed on the male provider, Coptic men don't marry until they are well-established. Usually, this means that they marry between 30 and 40, though nowadays many young men are able to marry in their late twenties. Young ladies are expected to marry before they reach the age of 25.

With marriage, the crucial dividing line is drawn between

Copts and Moslems. All the pressures of parental loyalty,
family conditioning, and social ostracism work against intermarriage as do the fundamental differences between Coptic
and Moslem marriages. Though the Moslems seldom marry
more than one wife and the government is attempting to
restrict divorce, the Moslem emphasis on easy divorce and
the right to marry more than one woman makes the Coptic
and Moslem views of marriage incompatible. This fortifies
the dividing line, for minorities that intermarry freely with
majorities soon disappear.

Each new marriage partnership then takes up its primary
function of raising a family and transmitting Coptic values
and attitudes. The cycle of Coptic replenishment moves forward; the indelible label is imposed on each child. In their
intimate involvement with their parents, the children are
swept into a larger involvement with the community of
Copts. Just as they may leave the church and remain in the
community, Copts leaving Egypt and the community still
remain loyal to their families. This is the bond that still is
evident in meeting dispersed Copts at a university campus
in Beirut, a restaurant in Rome, an apartment in Brooklyn.
In some cases, the complaints about lack of opportunity in
Egypt are transferred to the next generation. Copts say
that they never would have left "if we felt our children had
a future in Egypt." Their departure was a practical transaction. In exchange for the almost certain loss of Coptic
identity by sons and grandsons who would grow up with dim
consciousness that they are Copts and eventually disappear
by intermarriage into the new environment, the dispersed
Copts have purchased a future outside Egypt. Even in that
irretrievable final step, it can be said that they are acting on
behalf of the family by meeting what they regard as a responsibility to the next generation.

CHAPTER XVI
Majority vs. Minority

A minority can be sentenced to death by the majority or it can commit suicide as an identifiable group by assimilating. By fleeing or being expelled, it can escape either fate, but at a high price. In the forseeable future, the Copts face none of these possibilities; neither Moslem majority nor Coptic minority shows signs of resorting to such extreme solutions of Egypt's enduring minority problem. After each of these possibilities is disposed of quickly in summary fashion, a fundamental conflict remains between the minority's goal of a pluralistic society and the majority's policy of domination.

Even those Copts who recall with bitterness and anxiety the belligerence of the fanatical Moslem Brotherhood regard organized persecution, extermination or expulsion from Egypt as far-fetched nightmares. Any apprehension stems from the discomforting tendency of Egyptian nationalism to feed on scapegoats and from the fact that most non-Moslems have left Egypt—except for the Copts. The Suez crisis removed the last traces of British and French influence as well as their nationals; the other resident foreigners have not been far behind. Only a handful of Egyptian Jews re-

main, their symbol a lonely synagogue on Adly Pasha Street
that all Cairo passes without noticing. The invisible bogey-
men of colonialism, imperialism and Zionism persist in the
sound and fury of Egyptian propaganda, but increasingly
they resemble the repetitious sounds of a cracked phono-
graph record. The regime, facing a trying period filled with
frustrations as performance lags behind grandiose promises,
could seek new distractions and new scapegoats. Now that
Egypt has become a single-minority country, the Copts stand
alone, absorbing all the anxieties and frustrations of the
dominant majority.

Nonetheless, nightmares about expulsion of Copts or organized persecution remain far-fetched. Even the Moslem
Brothers acknowledged that the Copts have an ineradicable
Egyptian birthright. This has been consistently affirmed in
the "semantic" equality accorded them in Egyptian Constitutions and official speeches. The Nasser regime is devoid of
any racist theories, which would sound strange indeed in a
country whose people have been conditioned during generations of outside rule to believe in their own inferiority. At
the height of Egyptian ill-feeling toward Israel and the West
and during the expulsions of foreigners, there were few
atrocities and they were isolated instances. The regime has
also vigorously stamped out the threat of mob violence of
the kind that burned Cairo in January 1952. Finally, any
overt suppression of a native minority would undermine
Egypt's image-building in Africa and Asia as a champion of
the oppressed.

The Copts, for their part, demonstrate resistance to assimilation with the renewed vigor of church and community,
the solidity of family life, the implacable opposition to
intermarriage. Proud of their self-images as the "true Egyptians" and the "original Christians," the Copts are re-enforcing their label rather than surrendering to what they
consider the inferior Moslem way of life. While more Copts

might quit Egypt if there were a place to go, this would hardly affect the bulk of the minority. Moreover, since Egypt won't permit departing Copts to take their personal wealth with them, a practical handicap is added to psychological reluctance.

Determined both to remain in Egypt and to retain their identity, the Copts have had the same goal and the same complaint throughout this century. In the early 1900's, Kyriakos Mikhail, a Coptic journalist sent to London to arouse the sympathy of British public opinion, set down the unchanging goal: "We have asked for justice and equality with Egyptians and for full participation in the fruits which have resulted from the new regime." And the unchanging complaint: "The Copt has already lost much of his former position in Egypt; he is daily in danger of losing the little that remains." Both statements still apply as the Copts set their sights on harmonious coexistence between the many and the strong (the Moslems) and the weak and the skilled (the Copts). They seek a pluralistic society where cultural, religious and social diversity thrives but does not penalize the minority, yet unlike the typical beleaguered minority, the Copts are not trying to overcome feelings of inferiority or lower social status. Their deprivation is relative, their touchstone of dissatisfaction the immediate past.

The Copts are also victims of their own feelings of persecution. Sir John Bowring, the English writer and political economist, noted in the nineteenth century that the ruling Turks regarded the Copts as the "pariahs of the Egyptian people, yet they are an amiable, pacific, and intelligent race, whose worst vices have grown out of their seeking shelter from wrong and robbery." The Moslems have imposed a self-fulfilling prophecy on the Copts by regarding them as fanatics. Feeling cornered, the Copts struggle to protect themselves, intensifying clannishness and increasing their unrest and dissatisfaction. A chicken-and-egg cycle goes on uninterrupted: the Copts feel persecuted, the Moslems cite Coptic sensitivity, the Copts strain to overcome discrimination, the Moslems indict Coptic aggressiveness.

Faced with contracting opportunities, the Copts have often pursued a policy which implicitly contradicts their goal of a society in which religious labels do not determine access to power and success. They have demanded proportional guarantees for Copts in government, business and the universities. Having confirmed that the race is rigged, they sought a guaranteed share in the pre-determined outcome.

Moslem domination has previously been dramatized in terms of village life and documented in the distribution of prerogatives, positions and privilege. It presents a naked contradiction between the Coptic goal of equality for all Egyptians regardless of religion and the de facto Moslem policy that the Christian minority must be kept in its place. In the polarization of Coptic goals and Moslem policy, the elements of present and future conflict reside, and as in any struggle, fortune smiles on the strong.

At about the same time that a Coptic priest was describing in Upper Egypt what decisive leadership by President Nasser could do to improve majority-minority relations, the text for the occasion was supplied in Los Angeles by the then-presidential nominee of the Democrats, John F. Kennedy:

Only the President, the representative of all interests and all sections, can create the understanding and tolerance which is necessary if we are to make an orderly transition to a completely free society. If the President does not himself wage the struggle for equal rights, if he stands above the battle, then the battle will inevitably be lost.

In Egypt, President Nasser has ignored any Coptic demands for equal rights as he moves ahead toward a new society clearly different than that of the United States or England. In the wake of Syria's breaking away from the United Arab Republic, a committee of 250 was appointed to work on the format for Egypt's version of "Arab socialism." The Copts were once again a glaring omission. New York "Times" correspondent Jay Walz wrote from Cairo in December 1961:

The maroon and white turbans of Imams, religious leaders, dot the committee's assembly chamber. Mr. Nasser has referred several times to socialism as practiced by the Companions of the Prophet Mohammed. Some observers believe that Mr. Nasser is looking for an Islamic version of the late nineteenth-century Christian socialism of Europe. They believe, though, that Mr. Nasser would deny this, as he would any suggestion he is "importing ideology" from anywhere—or that his ideas are not 100 percent Islamic. A notable omission from all his discussion has been any reference to Christian Copts, whose 4,000,000 members represent one-sixth of the population of Egypt.

Unmistakably, the current regime in Egypt has selected the Pan-Islamic brand of Arab nationalism that recognizes only Moslems as full members of the nation. The Copts are placed in the position of guests for whom a place is set and a room provided in the house of Egypt. But the menu and the rules of hospitality are determined by the Moslem heads of the household. The alternate approach toward Arab nationalism, which was promoted during the Moslem-Coptic era of cooperation in opposing the British and in launching an independent country, separated religion and nationalism. It was directed toward a secular state, the happiest home for a religious minority.

Meanwhile, Islam itself is in ferment as it tries to adjust to the modern world and as its religious grip is weakened. The more educated, urbanized and modernized the Moslem Egyptian the less religious. This was reflected in a survey described by sociologist Daniel Lerner, who reported that farmers visited their mosque daily but none of the urban workers did. Three out of four urban workers went to the mosque once a week or less, the fourth never. While 89 per-

cent of the farmers preferred Koran readings on the radio,
the percentages declined with workers (64%), white collar
employees (38%) and professionals (28%).

Impassioned lip service to Islam persists, but it is no answer to modern problems, though it does affirm the Moslem's allegiance to his community, its strength paralleling
the Copt's allegiance to his community.

As modernizing Moslems struggle to remove the religious
straitjacket of traditionalists whose stronghold is al-Azhar
University, the unresolved crisis of Islam and modernism
probably will overshadow Nasser's political manipulations
of Mohammed's message. Indeed, Nasser may indirectly ac-
celerate the secular process by making political use of a religious instrument. From the Coptic viewpoint, any changes
taking place in Islam will affect relations with the Moslems,
with Coptic pessimists envisioning a Moslem state conditioned by the Koran and the optimists expecting a rein-
vigorated Coptic identity to thrive regardless of the outcome
of political, social and religious ferment within Islam. The
majority remains the obsessive, external reality even though
the Moslems don't return the attention. As the regime's ban
on any dialogue of accommodation between Copt and Moslem
makes their relations elusive, the Coptic obsession becomes
increasingly one-sided.

By making contact with the mainstream of Christianity
and by developing international affiliations, the Copts have
made it more difficult for any Egyptian regime to attack the
Coptic Church without repercussions. In 1961, the Coptic
Church sent delegations to the World Council of Churches
assembly in India and to the Greek Orthodox meeting on
the island of Rhodes. The Patriarch's chief advisor, Abuna
Makari as-Suriani, has been active in international assemblies since his attendance in 1954 at the World Council of
Churches assembly in Evanston, Ill., and subsequently has
attended various conferences in Europe as well as World

Council assemblies. As long as external propaganda remains important to the Egyptian government, the Copts have a potential weapon of counter-attack in case of extreme need: a single speech of complaint before an international assembly, with accompanying press coverage, would even make President Nasser pay attention to the cry of the Copts.

Early in 1962, shortly after the Coptic Patriarch entertained the head of the Anglican Church in Germany and a Protestant church dignitary from Upsala, Sweden, he sent a Coptic priest as his personal envoy on a tour of France, Belgium, the Netherlands, Switzerland, Austria, Denmark, England and Germany. Lecturing, making public appearances, baptizing and marrying dispersed Copts as he went, the priest followed on the heels of a correspondent from the Coptic weekly, "Watani," who reported during a lecturing and reporting tour that the Germans are "eager to learn about the Coptic Church." German newspapers published articles about the Copts and the Coptic Institute was asked to supply more information and to send a lecturer on tour. In Switzerland, the government donated a parcel of land for the building of a Coptic church in response to a request from Coptic university students in Zurich. The development of popular interest in Germany, where scholarly work on the Copts is already going on, has the strategic value of bringing the Copts to the attention of a country whose favor Egypt has always prized.

In Africa, where Egypt is focusing its attention, the Coptic Church has growing appeal as the continent's indigenous Christian church. Long the official religion of Ethiopia, which was converted in the fourth century, Coptic Christianity is attracting attention in East and South Africa, particularly in Kenya and Uganda. In South Africa, 400 native families belonging to a non-affiliated church have joined the Coptic Church en masse—their services in the

Coptic language, their sermons in Bantu and Zulu, their chief priest a Coptic monk.

With the signing of the Protocol of June 25, 1959, relations between the Churches of Egypt and Ethiopia were solidified, reaffirming the primacy of the Egyptian Patriarch, and specifying that an Ethiopian monk should head his country's branch of the Coptic Church. The head of the Ethiopian Church, who must be approved by Emperor Haile Selassie, was raised to the rank of Patriarch, a "second position in standing after the [Egyptian] Pope." All Ethiopian bishops and archbishops must pledge "to revere the Pope of Alexandria, Patriarch of the See of St. Mark, successor to the Evangelist St. Mark, and to consider him our Pope."

The Ethiopians, dissatisfied with the practice of appointing an Egyptian archbishop to head their church, were thereby mollified and their religious allegiance to the Egyptian Patriarch assured. During World War II, the Egyptian archbishop in Addis Ababa had committed the unforgiveable sin of blessing the Italian troops who were occupying Ethiopia. The Protocol marked the healing of that wound and blocked an incipient movement to break away from the Egyptian Church.

Though Egyptian Copts have a special attachment to Ethiopia and its emperor that is reciprocated, few have migrated to Ethiopia and no one takes seriously the occasional references to it as a refuge. The emperor's picture remains one of three pictures that invariably hang in Coptic institutions; the other two are of President Nasser and St. George killing the dragon. Ethiopia's Conquering Lion of Judah personally opened the Ethiopic section of the Coptic Museum and donated many items on exhibit, while the Coptic Institute stresses its program of Ethiopic studies. The Emperor, who periodically makes symbolic gifts to the Patriarch, delighted the Copts during an Egyptian state visit a few years ago by ceremoniously attending Mass in St. Mark's Cathedral and visiting the Coptic churches in Old Cairo. A prominent Copt who is close to the Emperor noted that the Coptic part of his state visit had to be added by the Emperor after it was omitted by the Egyptian Foreign Ministry. However, Ethiopia's increasingly friendly relations with Israel have added an uncomfortable sidelight to Haile Selassie's vigorous espousal of the Coptic Church.

Nonetheless, these external gestures are only a sideshow to the inescapable confrontation between the Coptic minority and the Moslem majority within the framework of a developing Egypt. As the majority policy of domination frustrates the minority goal of a pluralistic society, few Copts entertain serious hopes for a working partnership in which the "fruits of the regime" are available to all Egyptians without distinction. At present, the Copts would settle for limited participation, especially the opportunity to develop their talents and market their skills. It is a small favor they ask of Egypt and in return they are ready to serve in a nation replete with reminders of past Coptic services. In the Finance Ministry, for instance, only a Copt is likely to notice the portrait of one Toubia Camel-Toueg Pasha, a Copt like so many others who distinguished themselves. The pasha died in 1925, but his portrait has lingered on through eras of kings and colonels, a fading place of honor for the highly-respected Under-Secretary of State in the Ministry of Finance. Insofar as his grandchildren despair of rising in his footsteps, the Copts feel that this commitment to Egypt has been betrayed, the nation deprived of valuable services, and a burden of injustice borne by the new Egyptian in the making.

In an Egypt that is in transition and rushing to modernize under Nasser (or another), the Copts persist as a standing challenge as well as an under-utilized national resource. Both Egypt and Islam, like all other countries and ways of life in the modern world, must meet the test of toleration.

For Islam it is a moral challenge spread over its proverbial range from the Atlantic to the Indian Oceans. Citing its theoretical toleration does not silence the cry of its minorities. For a Moslem nation, it is the practical problem of using human resources.

The Copts themselves, within the microcosm of their history and its manifestations in church, community, nation and minority, present everyman's tale of dream and nightmare, fulfillment and frustration in a world not of their making. Insofar as the Copts have received their due—without ignoring their blemishes—this modern story of Egypt's Copts is an account of the human condition.

At the end of this intimate rendezvous with the Copts, a concluding moral note is unavoidable. The obligation to oppose tyranny stands even when the tyranny is elusive and unannounced, even unintended. It begins with labeling injustice long before shop windows are smashed, icons broken, and families torn apart. This labeling is an antidote to the danger of dulled sensibilities in our time and while the Copts can be accused of hypersensitivity, their problem is by no means imaginary. They are feeling pressures that inflict suffering without mutilating, that intimidate relentlessly without exploding sporadically, that wound without bloodshed.

The Copts are numbed and helpless as well as anxious as their historic cycles of acceptance and rejection, their recurring stages of toleration, discrimination and persecution move inexorably in the direction of rejection. Persecution is still the nightmare, discrimination the reality in the latest chapter of a long story of a people. They are there in Egypt and there they remain, the "true Egyptians," the "original Christians," the four million Copts of the Nile Valley, that troubled, enduring, lonely minority.

INDEX

Abdel Malik, Gindi, 96, 98
Akladios, Dr. Bahour Labib, 155
Antoun, Farid, 81, 83–84, 89–90
Assimilation, 5, 167, 168
Attulah, Dr. Wahib, 131, 145
Awda, Abdel Qadir, 81–84, 90
al-Azhar, 19, 54, 62, 78–79, 172
al-Bakury, Sheikh Ahmed Hassan, Minister of Waqfs, 51, 53, 55

Baptism, 44, 161
Bishops, Holy Synod of, 98, 99–100, 105–106, 107, 150, 151
Boulos, Abuna Boulos, 143–146
British occupation, 14–17
Butcher, Mrs. E. L., 28, 106, 159

Catholics in Egypt, 25, 61, 100, 139
Census of Copts, 23–25
Christians in Egypt, 21, 25–26, 51–52, 155–156
Clergy, 12–13, 95, 130–133, 140–146
Constitutional guarantees, 56, 168
Conversion, 7–8, 12–13, 26, 49, 83–87, 89, 135–136, 139–140
Coptic calendar, 7, 32
Coptic Community Council, 9, 29, 98, 102, 105–106, 107, 147–154
Coptic Congress of 1911, 16–17
Coptic Institute (Catholic), 139
Coptic language, 8, 13, 153–154, 155, 158
Coptic Museum, 155, 174
Coptic Seminary, 131–133, 143, 145, 152
Coptic welfare groups, 157–159
Copts in government, 9–10, 17, 43–46, 57, 62–63, 71, 175
Council of Chalcedon, 6, 125
Courtship and marriage, 85, 163–166
Crime, 22
Cromer, Lord, 11, 15
Cross as a symbol, 3, 5, 43, 136–138

Divorce, 22–23, 49, 83–84, 88, 89, 166

Durrell, Lawrence, xi, 23

Ebeid, Makram, 17, 20
Education, 27, 64–65, 68–70
Emigration, 5, 31, 37–38, 160, 166, 167, 169, 174
Employment, 26–29, 37, 46–49
Ethiopian Church, 116, 173–174

Family life, 11–12, 22–23, 161–162
Fasting, 127

Gabra, Dr. Sami, 155
Ghali, Butros, 71, 148
Gorst, Sir Eldon, 16
Government positions, 43–47, 48–49
Government relations with Copts, 20, 24–25, 32–34, 38–39, 44–49, 50–56, 57–59, 61, 63–70, 74, 79–80, 99–101, 106–107, 151–152, 168, 170–171, 173

Haile Selassie, 94, 174–175
Higher Institute of Coptic Studies, 13, 139, 152, 155–156, 173, 174
Hosny, Ahmed, 100–101
Hussein, Kamal Eddine, 63, 65–67

"Images," 24
Israel, 54–55, 175

Jews in Egypt, 52–53, 167–168

Lerner, Daniel, 171
Liberation Province, 47–48
Luka, Nazmi, 65–67

Maglis Milli. See Coptic Community Council
"al-Manarat," 19–20
Martyrs and Martyrdom, 7, 34, 129
al-Maskin, Abuna Matta, 111, 123–124, 141
Meinardus, Dr. Otto, 109, 111, 121
Mikhail, Kyriakos, 15–16, 169
Millet system, 8–9, 82–83, 148
"Misr," 19, 101, 157

Nazerenes, Ra'stas

Jamaicans 'the scattered'

diaspora 'In the Black'

CPSIA information can be obtained at www.ICGtesting.com
Printed in the USA
BVOW03s1052060415

394876BV00001B/53/P